COLD HARD TRUTH ON

MEN, WOMEN & MONEY

COLD HARD TRUTH ON

MEN, WOMEN

& MONEY

COLD HARD TRUTH ON
MEN, WOMEN & MONEY

50 COMMON MONEY MISTAKES AND HOW TO FIX THEM

KEVIN O'LEARY

G

GALLERY BOOKS

NEW YORK   LONDON   TORONTO   SYDNEY   NEW DELHI

NOTE TO READERS

This publication contains the opinions and ideas of its author. It is sold with the understanding that neither the author nor the publisher is engaged in rendering legal, tax, investment, insurance, financial, accounting, or other professional advice or services. If the reader requires such advice or services, a competent professional should be consulted. Relevant laws vary from state to state. The strategies outlined in this book may not be suitable for every individual, and are not guaranteed or warranted to produce any particular results.

No warranty is made with respect to the accuracy or completeness of the information contained herein, and both the author and the publisher specifically disclaim any responsibility for any liability, loss or risk, personal or otherwise, which is incurred as a consequence, directly or indirectly, of the use and application of any of the contents of this book.

G

Gallery Books
A Division of Simon & Schuster, Inc.
1230 Avenue of the Americas
New York, NY 10020

First Gallery Books paperback edition July 2014

GALLERY BOOKS and colophon are registered trademarks of Simon & Schuster, Inc.

For information about special discounts for bulk purchases, please contact Simon & Schuster Special Sales at 1-866-506-1949 or business@simonandschuster.com.

The Simon & Schuster Speakers Bureau can bring authors to your live event. For more information or to book an event, contact the Simon & Schuster Speakers Bureau at 1-866-248-3049 or visit our website at www.simonspeakers.com.

Designed by Kyoko Watanabe

Manufactured in the United States of America

10 9 8 7 6 5 4 3 2 1

ISBN 978-1-4767-3442-2
ISBN 978-1-4767-3444-6 (tp)
ISBN 978-1-4767-3445-3 (ebook)

I dedicate this book to my wife, Linda, who married me when I had nothing and taught me that family is senior to everything on life's balance sheet.

CONTENTS

INTRODUCTION: **Money Problems Are Financial
Opportunities**   1

PART ONE:
SPEND LESS, SAVE WELL,
INVEST OFTEN

1. **Money Lessons I Learned from My Mother**   9
   Spending, Saving, Investing: A Personal-Finance Quiz

2. **Your 90-Day Number**   19
   Cold Hard Truth Card

3. **Save Your Money, Save Your Life**   37
   Reviving Ghost Money

4. **Invest Right, Invest Now**   51
   5 Investment Rules to Live By

5. **Debt-Free First**   67
   Money Pledge

Contents

PART TWO:

YOUTH AND MONEY: LEARNING & EARNING, DATING & MATING

6. Kids and Cash   77
   Test Your Child's Money Smarts

7. The High Cost of Higher Education   105
   Quiz: Are You Ready for the High Cost of Higher Ed?

8. Boomers and Boomerangs: When Generations
   Financially Collide   123
   10 Steps for Getting Your Kid Out of Your Basement

9. Young Love and Money   133
   10 Financial Questions to Ask Your Partner Before You
   Move In Together

PART THREE:

MARRIAGE, MORTGAGE, AND CHILDREN

10. Marriage and Money   147
    Get Hitched and Stay Rich: 10 Ways to Minimize
    Wedding-Spending Madness

11. House Poor, House Rich   165
    10 Ways to Renovate Smarter

Contents

12. **Cash in the Cradle**   185
    5 Ways to Minimize Baby-Spending Madness

13. **Avoiding Money Pits**   193
    4 More Money Pits to Avoid

PART FOUR:
MIDLIFE MONEY MATTERS & YOUR FINANCIAL LEGACY

14. **Midlife and Money Karma**   207
    Measure Your Midlife Money Karma

15. **Divorce, Remarriage, and Gold Diggers**   219
    How to Spot a Gold Digger

16. **Debt, Divesting, and Downsizing**   229
    10 Crucial Financial Questions You Must Ask about
    Late-in-Life Care

EPILOGUE: **Getting to "Enough"**   247

ACKNOWLEDGMENTS   249

ABOUT THE AUTHOR   251

AUTHOR'S NOTE

This book is the story of my money, and the personal journey I went on to make it. None of the content, anecdotes, stories, opinions, or recollections contained in this book should be construed as investment advice, especially as they relate to any financial products I may represent. Investors should speak with their financial advisors for any investment advice and to discuss the risks of investing in any financial product. This book represents my personal opinions and should be enjoyed as such. Please note that names and identifying details of some of the people portrayed in this book have been changed.

COLD HARD TRUTH ON
MEN, WOMEN
& MONEY

Money Problems Are Financial Opportunities

It was a Saturday afternoon in April when I was stopped on the street by an older, well-put-together woman in Beacon Hill, an upscale neighborhood in the heart of Boston. She looked like she'd lived a very good life and was enjoying this latest chapter in relative ease and comfort. I figured she was heading for a pricey lunch with some equally posh friends. Good for her, I thought. But even before she began to speak, I noticed something. She was smiling, but there was something unsettled about her expression.

We began to talk about a recent pitch she'd watched on *Shark Tank*. After a bit more conversation, she felt comfortable enough to scold me a little over an onscreen tiff I'd had with Barbara Corcoran. Then, she leaned in a little closer, changing the topic.

"I was wondering if I couldn't ask for a bit of advice from you, Kevin," she said.

Never one to shy away from sharing my opinions, I said, "Shoot." I figured she was going to ask about a stock drop or a new retirement vehicle. But her concerns were far more personal than that. She told me her husband had passed away months earlier and she was beginning to feel increasingly overwhelmed by mounting financial responsibilities, ones she'd never shouldered before. Suddenly, this woman who had lived in financial comfort into her sixties found herself having trouble getting her own credit card. Everything she had before was in her husband's name. Beyond that, she found herself in charge of paying bills for the first time, but had no idea how to scrutinize them for errors or hidden costs. She spent the same amount of money she always had—"Too much," she said—but had no idea what her balances were at the end of the month. "Should I sell my house, Kevin, and downsize? Or should I hold on to it?" she asked. Her family was beginning to pester her about the estate. She had two grandchildren in college she wanted to help, and her sister was angling for a loan for a small business. She knew her late husband had had some investments, but she wasn't sure what they were in and whether they were doing well or not. Mostly, she was worried about the economy and what that would mean to the nest egg she knew her husband had socked away somewhere. My alarm bells went off. I thought about my own wife, Linda. Would she know how to manage our finances if something happened to me? I doubted it.

This woman in Beacon Hill was far from destitute. She had the means, but had never learned anything about how to manage her own personal finances. She was scared and she was alone.

Tears welled in her eyes. If she'd been pitching me on *Shark Tank*, I would have said, "Pull yourself together. Your tears don't add any value." In business, money and emotions don't mix. But this woman wasn't asking me for money. She wasn't pitching me an idea. She was asking me for help. And I wanted to give it to her.

2

I tried to gather a bit more information. "How are you getting your money now?" I asked.

"A check from our investments comes every month as a direct deposit. And then there's another automatic deposit that arrives in our account once a month—I'm just not sure where it's coming from. I use my bank card to make withdrawals from our accounts. I'm so embarrassed by how little I know about our finances."

"Have you talked to your bank manager?"

"Yes, but I don't really understand what he's telling me. I've never been very good with money, which is why my husband used to take care of things."

"And why are you asking me for help?"

"I guess because I trust you to tell me the truth."

I leaned toward her as though delivering the most important information she'd ever receive. "I want you to listen to me very carefully," I said. "Until you know exactly where you stand financially, until you have a crystal-clear picture of your money situation—your flow in and out, your expenses, your savings, your investments, everything, and you consult an expert—you are to give away NO money. None. Not to your grandchildren, not to your siblings. Not a dime. Do you understand?"

She nodded, still fighting back tears. This woman needed someone reliable to go through her accounts and write up an intuitive financial plan that would be simple for her to follow and guarantee that her money would outlast her. I gave her my card and the number of a good friend of mine who was a rock-solid financial advisor, and I told her to stay in touch.

As I walked away, I wasn't feeling very good about the exchange. I shuddered to think how easily it can all go wrong for someone who has no money sense, even when she has money.

One tough market correction, one bad loan, one ill-advised investment, and all that money could disappear. Who would take care of this woman then?

The inspiration for this book came from that moment, a casual conversation on a street corner with someone in need asking me for help with her personal finances. Though people have always sought out my investment advice, I've never billed myself as a personal-finance expert. But I *am* a money expert. For that reason, this book is going to be different from other books that offer financial advice. This book isn't just about money, but about your relationship with money. I've always believed that if you improve how you relate to money, you'll have more of it. I'm going to show why that's true, and how to build financial stability by thinking differently about your finances.

My goal is simple: to offer practical ways for you to save money, invest better, and cut your costs—at every stage in life, from cradle to grave. I'll teach you how to raise money-savvy kids who don't spend too much or get into debt too early. I'll show you how young people can graduate with less debt and in better shape to pay off student loans. I'll show you how to talk to your loved ones about money and how to make sure your romantic relationships, marriages, and partnerships don't get overshadowed by debt, overspending, and financial concerns. I'll help you avoid common mistakes people make with credit and credit cards, when buying a house or a car, or when blowing a fortune on luxury goods that don't appreciate over time. But most of all, I'll guide you through all of life's stages and decision points, helping you get to a place in your twilight years where money and freedom can result in comfort and security. Are you ready to embark on this journey with me? Then let's get started.

Here's the cold hard truth: No matter how much money you make, the world is designed to take it away. Right from the day you're born, your money is under siege. As soon as your parents put you in the cradle, the bank will encourage them to open a 529 college-savings plan to fund your future. That's probably the same bank you'll start paying fees to when you open your first checking account a few years down the line. Time passes, you grow up, and eventually, you're off to college. There's the bank again, giving you a hefty student loan. And then your first credit card. And after you graduate and get married, the bank offers you a massive mortgage. Then it scares you into buying unnecessary insurance policies. Later, it might coerce you into buying an annuity or other complicated financial products stuffed with hidden fees. Student loans, credit cards, and mortgages are powerful financial tools that are necessary if you want to live a full, well-rounded life. But you can see how easy it is for the average person who doesn't understand how these tools work, like the woman I met in Beacon Hill, to make big money mistakes. Don't let that be you. I'm here to help you avoid her fate.

It starts by waking up to the truth about your financial situation. By doing that, you'll begin using clearheaded reasoning instead of emotions when making money decisions. And that alone will change the way you relate to money.

All the time, I am asked this question: "Kevin, what is the secret to becoming wealthy?" Here it is—the secret:

Don't spend too much. Mostly save. Always invest.

Simple advice is often easy to swallow but hard to follow. If it weren't, I could end this book right here! After all, I've just given you all the information you need to become wealthier and retire in comfort. Why, then, is it so hard to follow the advice above? Why do so many people do the opposite—invest poorly, spend way too much, save almost nothing, and remain willfully ignorant about their finances? *Because they don't understand their relationship to money.* In fact, they fear understanding it because they find it daunting—or in some cases, they fear knowledge because it might mean making changes to their financial lives.

The fact is, more money isn't going to fix anything if your relationship to money is damaged. You won't find any "automatic millionaires" in these pages. Sometimes more money simply means digging an even deeper debt hole. But no matter how much money you have, I'm going to help you keep more of it for yourself. After all, the point of having more money isn't the money itself, but the freedom that money can buy you.

Part One

SPEND LESS, SAVE WELL, INVEST OFTEN

Me in San Francisco in 1984 in the early days of SoftKey Software
Products. We were losing money every day. I was scared out of
my mind. I know a thing or two about feeling financial loss.
(Property of Kevin O'Leary)

CHAPTER 1

Money Lessons I Learned from My Mother

In the same way that our relationship to food is shaped by lessons learned during childhood, so, too, is our relationship with money. It is often our parents, for better or for worse, who teach us our first money lessons. My mother, Georgette, was a master with money. She was born in Montreal to parents of Lebanese descent. And while she didn't have a fancy business degree, she was thrust into the family clothing business at a very young age, after the sudden death of her father. In the Lebanese culture, businesses are usually passed down to the boys, but her brother, Norman, was too young to take over. So in the beginning, it was up to my mother and her sister to keep the business running until Norman was old enough to take over. Turns out, my mom was a natural at balancing the books. She met my father, Terry, through the family business. He was a charismatic guy and one of the company's most talented salesmen—until his personal problems meant he lost every penny he earned.

Many marriages crash against the unforgiving shores of bad

money management, and too often children bear the brunt of their parents' financial decisions. My parents shielded my brother, Shane, and me from the worst of their marital woes, but my mother's marriage to my father broke down largely over money matters. He was good to Shane and me, but he was a fun-loving Irishman who liked to buy rounds at the bar and gamble with his friends.

I was six years old when my mother was granted sole custody of Shane and me. She got remarried, to a man named George Kanawaty, who became a father figure to Shane and me—something my own father couldn't be because of his addictions. After the wedding, we all moved to Illinois so that my new step-father could pursue a Ph.D. in business. One day, fed up with the custody arrangement, my birth father threatened to come to Champaign-Urbana and bring Shane and me back with him. My mother had heard he'd fallen in with a rough crowd, so she didn't want us going there. The plan was for my mom and both of us kids to fly to Europe for as long as it took George to reason with my dad in Illinois. But the trip required cashing in a big part of George and my mother's emergency savings, which weren't significant to begin with. When my mother married George, he was a student with $36 to his name.

Where there's a will, there's a way—and I have never met a woman with more will than my mother. The three of us flew to Lausanne, Switzerland, where my brother and I would be safe. After waiting it out for weeks in a foreign hotel room with two little children, and despite her determination and cool resolve, my mother finally burst into tears. She was at the end of her rope, in terms of both stress and finances. The money that was keeping her children safe from a man she didn't trust to take care of them was running out. And both George and my mother had used up almost all of their resources. There was nowhere else to turn. Kids pick up every nuance of parental strife and store it in a place so deep in their subconscious that it affects them for the rest of their lives. I knew George and my mother didn't have the money to hire expensive lawyers to fight this in court, and they certainly couldn't afford to keep us hidden in Europe forever. I will never forget my mother's fear, the look on her face when she realized that eventually the money would run out and she might lose her children.

Less than eight weeks into our exile, sadly, tragically, my father died of a heart attack at the age of thirty-seven. The custody struggle was over. Still, our precarious financial situation, and my mother's panic about it, moved through my bloodstream in that one moment, and I think it changed my very DNA. I remember thinking, *I never want to feel this frightened and powerless again. I never want my own children to experience economic terror.* Early-childhood trauma is an awful thing, but in this case, it might have been an odd blessing for me. Looking back, I think that's when the seeds of my own need to achieve financial security were sown.

Maybe you're wondering why I'm telling you this story. The truth is that when I deliver tough-minded financial advice, I want you to know where it comes from. I'm a wealthy man now, but at various points in my life, I've experienced the terror of economic insecurity firsthand. I've shared this personal story with you to show that sometimes in life, people may be able to help you out of difficult situations. But there are other times when the only thing that can help you is money. But for money to save you, first, you have to save it.

———————

Beyond saving money in case of catastrophe, my mother was also a savvy spender. Here's the distinction: She was careful with her money, but she wasn't cheap. I remember admiring a Chanel jacket she once wore to Christmas dinner at our place in Boston.

"Great jacket, Mom. Must have cost you a fortune."

"Not this year," she said.

"What do you mean?" I asked.

"Kevin, dear. This jacket is old. I've had it forever."

This surprised me because the jacket was so stylish and beautiful, a black classic box cut. It looked like she'd just picked it up off the rack from that season's new line, but she then told me she'd bought it in the late sixties, twenty years earlier! She spent, at the time, a small fortune—about $500—for that jacket. We didn't discuss this further, but knowing my mother, she would have saved and thought about this purchase for a long time before actually following through. She would have tried it on a few times, with George there to give her feedback. But the thing is, she wore that jacket for decades. She didn't dry-clean her clothes every time she wore them. She steamed them now and again, to maintain their shape and color. She never flung her clothes on the back of chairs. She always hung them up on hangers. Not everyone can afford Chanel, that must be said, but this example begs some serious math.

Let's say you buy a bargain black blazer at the Gap for $100. It'll probably stay in style for a season and pill and fade after dry cleaning it five to ten times. So in the course of twenty years of professional use, you'll purchase a new black blazer every two years, say, for a total of $1,000—assuming the price never goes higher than $100. Using the math above, you could say my mother's jacket, purchased for $500 more than twenty years earlier, saved her $500. But here's the real value: The perpetually fashionable Chanel blazer would fetch about $1,000 today, according to vintage clothing collectors I've consulted.

So who saved more money? You, with your $100 blazer purchased every two years for twenty years, at the cost of $1,000? Or my mother, who bought one jacket, once, at a price of $500, wore it for twenty years, then sold it for $1,000? I want you to know this is coming from a man who balks at a designer price tag. I can't believe how much good-quality clothes cost. And I also want to be very clear that *I'm not advocating that you go out and buy Chanel if you can't afford it.* But I am asking you, with everything you buy, to *consider value over impulse.* I am asking you to examine all your purchases and begin to treat everything you buy as an investment. Everything. Even a blazer. I want you to start thinking about quality and the potential resale value of every single purchase you make. It's a good discipline that will cut down on a lot of impulse and redundant spending.

That's what Georgette did. Incidentally, that's what my wife, Linda, does, too. We went to a black-tie function recently, and she pulled out a dress she's had for more than ten years. It's a classic cut, beautifully made, the kind of silhouette that never goes out of style. She's gotten a lot of use out of it. And while my mother bought some of the most beautiful and expensive clothes I've ever seen, almost none of what she bought lost much of its value or stylishness over time. Her closet was well curated. She never bought too much or overspent. She was a smart shopper. Incidentally, my daughter, Savannah, has become a vintage clothing hound. She buys a lot of great pieces secondhand. I like to think she inherited her unique style from her mother and her frugality from her grandmother.

In 2008, my beloved mother passed away. It was devastating

and unexpected: a heart attack followed by a stroke on the operating table. Days later, I was told that she had made me the executor of her estate. After years working for the United Nations,
she and George had enjoyed a textured life, rich in experiences,
travel, friends, and fine food, but their lifestyle was by no means
overly lavish. They mostly lived on George's solid UN income,
so my mother's money was hers to invest and spend. She never
merged it with her husband's. That money was all her own, and
George didn't even know how much she had. Keeping some
money separate for you and only you is one of the best financial
lessons I can impart to you. (I'll talk more about that and what I
call your "Secret 10" in Chapter 6.) But at the time of my mother's death, I hadn't given this idea much thought. Mostly, I never
imagined that Georgette's savings amounted to much. But when
I opened the books and studied her long-term investment portfolio, I got a big surprise. She'd amassed the kind of nest egg with
which most people could enjoy a worry-free, exciting retirement.
By the looks of her portfolio activity, she mostly invested and
rarely spent. She didn't set aside considerable chunks of cash, just
a steady amount every month, and only in *stocks or securities
that paid her a dividend or a yield.*

When people talked about investing like this, I always thought
they were talking about another era. But do you have any idea
what happens to a portfolio over forty years that contains only
bonds with interest and stocks with dividends? You have to see
it to believe it. My mother's portfolio was a sweeping, arcing
line tracing value over time—it only went up—and her balance
steadily grew and multiplied at an incredible rate. When I analyzed my mother's secret cache, when I studied her slow and
steady investment style and the healthy nest egg she'd tucked
away for herself, here's what I learned: With very little money

I received this Warhol-like canvas as a gift from
a friend who said I was "obsessed by money."
I took it as a compliment! This now hangs on
the wall at O'Leary Ventures Corporation.
(Artman Agency/Cyrille Margarit)

and a bit of expertise, anyone can grow his or her money. My
mother did it. So can you.

Spending, Saving, Investing: A Personal-Finance Quiz

To change your fortunes, abide by my mother's three simple
rules: *Don't spend too much. Mostly save. Always invest.* Before
we embark on this financial journey together, the most important tool you'll need is information—about yourself, your goals,
and your ability to achieve them. You have to know where
you're at before you head where you're going. To test your
self-knowledge about your own spending, saving, and investing

habits, try the quiz below. There are no wrong answers, only honest ones.

ON SPENDING

1. At any given time, do you know exactly how much money is in your wallet, your checking/investments/savings accounts? Y/N
2. Do you go shopping with a specific list, buying only what's on it with rare exceptions? Y/N
3. Do you refrain from putting consumer goods or groceries on a credit card, paying only in cash or with debit card unless absolutely necessary? Y/N
4. Do you resist last-minute purchases (such as magazines, chocolate bars, or gum) in the checkout aisle? Y/N
5. Do you research prices and comparatively shop before you hit the stores? Y/N
6. Do you skip or block the shopping channel at home to prevent making unnecessary purchases from your couch? Y/N
7. Do you pay off your credit cards at the end of the month, using them only for convenience or to gather reward points? Y/N
8. Do you keep your receipts carefully filed and promptly return items if you're less than satisfied with them or find you don't need them? Y/N
9. Are you aware of all available discounts, rebates, and coupons before making any purchases? Y/N
10. Are you able to avoid shopping when you're stressed, bored, worried, or tired? Y/N

ON SAVING

1. Do you set aside a certain amount every month for savings, never veering from these commitments unless it's an emergency? Y/N
2. Do you save money in the highest-interest savings account you can find? Y/N
3. Do you keep minimum balances to avoid paying bank fees? Y/N
4. Do you understand how much you're paying in banking fees? Y/N
5. Do you live within your means? Y/N
6. Do you make debt repayment a priority? Y/N
7. If you have children, do you have a plan in place to save for their education? Y/N
8. If you're planning to buy a house, are you saving for a sufficient down payment (at least 20 percent)? Y/N
9. Do you cultivate good habits—such as bringing lunch to work and using libraries—with the express purpose of saving money? Y/N
10. Do you have money set aside in case of emergencies? Y/N

ON INVESTING

1. Are you ready to invest? Y/N
2. Do you have a clear understanding of your retirement goals? Y/N
3. Do you understand your appetite for risk? Y/N
4. Do you have working knowledge of the various financial

products available to you, from stocks to bonds to treasuries to mutual funds, and the difference between yield, nonyield, dividend- and non-dividend-paying products? Y/N

5. Do you have a pension plan? Y/N
6. Do you understand retirement vehicles—IRAs, 401(k)s— and their attendant tax benefits? Y/N
7. Do you work with a trusted financial advisor who helps you navigate complicated investing vehicles? Y/N
8. Do you pay attention to financial news on a regular basis? Y/N
9. Do you invest only in things you understand? Y/N?
10. Do you react to volatile markets with moderation and patience? Y/N

If you answered yes to most of these questions, kudos to you. I hope this book reinforces some of your good spending, saving, and investment habits and helps you avoid forming bad ones.

If you've answered roughly half yes, half no, then these pages offer valuable advice to help you tip the scales back in favor of financial health.

If you answered no to most of these questions, *then you are heading for financial trouble.* But it's not too late to change; in fact, when it comes to money, it's never too late to change. Keep reading.

CHAPTER 2

Your 90-Day Number

The first step in changing money habits is taking a cold hard look at your financial input and output. Before you can redirect your money into savings and investments, you have to stanch the outward flow. That means getting a handle on your spending. Here's what I want you to do: I want you to boil your money matters down to one simple number. It's going to be either a positive or a negative number, because money is black and white. There is no gray. You either have it or you don't.

To get started, read the instructions below and use the charts provided. This shouldn't take you more than half an hour.

I hear a lot of groans. You're thinking this is like homework and you're just going to skip this part and keep reading, am I right? No! Don't do that. That's a really bad idea. If you're serious about changing your financial status, you need to do a bit of work. Businesses do this quarterly. In fact, I spend thousands of dollars *a month* to keep track of my personal and corporate accounts. And I've done this with every business I've ever been part of. A lack of vigilance can mean a company is suddenly teetering on the edge of bankruptcy because it's not monitoring its numbers closely or often enough. It happens that fast. I've seen it. And it's a hard lesson to learn. I will never allow a lack of diligence to affect any of my business holdings, which is why I'm offering you this advice about knowing your numbers. And this applies as much to a business as it does to your personal finances: Ignorance costs you money, and it's totally avoidable.

I like to catch anomalies in numbers before they become entrenched financial problems, big or small. For the past fifteen years, my wife has kept every single receipt for every single purchase she has made, and every few weeks we match those purchases with the credit card bill, allocating every item. It's just too easy to let hidden charges, overcharges, mistakes, or financial anomalies get lost in the shuffle, especially in your personal finances. Consider that a while ago, I received a call from my bookkeeper, who noticed a significant rise in our family phone bill. It went from being in the hundreds to almost $1,000—in one month! We discovered the increase was due to exorbitant roaming charges my son and I incurred while on vacation. We got a little too enthusiastic about our new iPhones and forgot that our plan did not cover roaming abroad. I'll refrain from ranting about the robbery of roaming charges, and after receiving that ridiculous bill, I certainly had an instructive chat about them with my son. Negotiating down that bill, which was the size of a pamphlet, wasn't easy. But if you're vigilant and watch where your money is going, you can plug the hole before your hard-earned cash disappears down the drain.

So have I convinced you? Are you ready to work on your financial picture?

Money Mistake: You're in the Dark About Your Finances

THE FIX: KNOW YOUR 90-DAY NUMBER

Knowledge is power. To know your spending and saving habits, start by adding up all your earnings over the course of three months. I call this your 90-Day Number. One month doesn't tell you much. Addiction specialists say it takes about a month to notice entrenched patterns of thinking and behavior and a couple more to introduce better ones. When a recovering addict comes to a crossroads, he or she is often advised to go to recovery meetings of some sort or another. And the person is told to go to 90 meetings in 90 days. I'm not saying you're addicted to spending—some of you may be, while many of you probably aren't. Either way, your 90-Day Number is going to give you valuable information about your spending and saving habits. If you've read this far, I'm assuming you want to change. So get out a pen and fill in the blanks below.

Start with your income. If you don't keep pay stubs, go back and look at your bank statements. Add up the column of all incoming money, automatically deposited paychecks, including any money you make on the side—even money the government might not know about. Include it all—the coins rolled and deposited, tax returns, money from cash jobs, returned bottles, eBay sales, lottery wins, baby bonuses, alimony or child support, money borrowed by or paid to you, dividends or interest earned on any investments that you do have. Don't include your assets, just the liquid stuff—the flow, the cash coming in. Write it all down.

MY PERSONAL MONEY PICTURE

90-Day Input

Income/Salary (Net)_____

Child Support_____

Alimony_____

Bonuses/Winnings_____

Tax Returns/Credits_____

Interest Earned_____

Dividends Earned_____

Employment Insurance_____

Annuities_____

Inheritances_____

Under-the-Table Income_____

eBay Sales_____

Other_____

Other_____

Other_____

Your 90-Day Input Number_____

Now, on a separate page, add up every single dollar you spend.
All outgoing money: every latte, every pair of shoes, every bag of

chips at every counter you've stood at while waiting for your car to come out of the car wash, every haircut, every donated coin, every lottery ticket, book, transit fare, tip, oil change, every ice cream cone bought for your kids, every movie ticket and parking ticket, that second glass of wine at a restaurant, that round-trip ticket, that first-class upgrade. Track all of it. Most important, document your debt payments, your bills and utilities, your car payments, and your mortgage or rent. You're looking for a pattern that 90 days of spending will begin to make clear. Write it all down.

90-Day Output

Rent/Mortgage Payments _____

Condo Fees/Property Taxes _____

Home Repair/Upkeep _____

Child Care _____

Dependent Care _____

Education _____

Alimony _____

Veterinarian _____

Health Care (medical) _____

Health Care (dental) _____

Prescriptions _____

Health Insurance _____

Gym _____

Cosmetics _____

Personal Care (salon/spa/yoga) _____

Pet Food/Expenses _____

Car/Lease Payments _____

Insurance (car/life/home) _____

Investments _____

Taxes _____

Debt Payments _____

Gifts _____

Car Repairs _____

Gas _____

Parking _____

Public Transit _____

Cabs _____

Utilities _____

Phone _____

Home Repairs/Services _____

Cable/Internet _____

Books/Magazines/Newspapers _____

Hobbies _____

Cold Hard Truth on Men, Women & Money

Clothing _____

Dry Cleaning_____

Groceries _____

Restaurants _____

Takeout _____

Travel _____

Entertainment/Movies/Concerts _____

Video Games _____

Computers/Repairs_____

Misc. Technology _____

Banking Fees_____

Legal/Accounting Fees _____

Home Office Supplies _____

Other_____

Other_____

Other_____

Other_____

Other_____

Other_____

Other_____

Other_____

Other_____

Your 90-Day Output Number _____

Now it's time for a dose of reality. In the space provided below, take your 90-Day Input Number and subtract from it your 90-Day Output Number.

Your 90-Day Input Number _____

Your 90-Day Output Number_____

Your 90-Day Number _____

Write that 90-Day Number down. Is it a positive number or a negative one? If you're taking in more money than you spend, congratulations! You're the rare person who has a positive financial outlook. Whatever you're doing, keep it up. Now, there's still the matter of maximizing your money's efficiency, eliminating uncertainties and putting that excellent surplus to better use—namely, saving for emergencies. I'll teach you how to do all of that in the chapters that follow. Those changes might be challenging at first, but you'll adjust, because you're starting from a place of strength and diligence.

If you don't fit the above profile, maybe you're someone with a number that comes up just slightly above zero. You're getting by with a little extra, especially if you have little saved. But you're not really in the clear. I worry about you because you may never have experienced rock bottom, so you're not really aware of how dangerously close you are to financial jeopardy. That's why I sometimes think that people who have experienced debt, people who have hit rock bottom, have a perverse kind of advantage over others: Their problems are so huge, they simply can't go on ignoring them. But what's best for you, in your current situation, is NOT to let things get worse and instead to get away from the growing cloud of financial insecurity you're so used to living under. You aren't really living within your means until you've saved three months' salary as a protective cushion, and that's on top of all other nonliquid assets. You may not see now that you're inches away from disaster, but I'm telling you the truth about what your 90-Day Number is revealing: You're just one major illness, one job loss, or one big market correction away from penury, or from losing your house, or worse. Time to make some changes. I'll help you do that.

Now, if you've done the math and your 90-Day Number is in the heavy negatives, then, like a majority of men and women out there, you simply spend more than you make. You're constantly operating in the red. It feels like you're living only to finance your debts or pay your bills. You are in constant fear of losing your job, or of your assets losing their value. You worry that one big, unexpected bill might put you under for good, and then you avoid that thought. You're avoiding the phone and people to whom you owe money. Maybe you're retreating from friends and family out of fear or shame. You're steeped in magical thinking about money—for example, believing you're one lottery ticket, inheritance, or windfall away from total financial transformation. You wake up in despair and you go to bed defeated. You don't live within your means because you don't even know what they are. You're *not* one illness, one job loss, one market correction, or one false move away from complete financial disaster. *Disaster is already here.*

If this is you, you must admit it to yourself now and take

every necessary step to correct it. Our understanding of money is formed early. But I believe people raised in poverty or with parents who severely mismanaged money can be at an advantage here. They know much more clearly what *not* to do with money; they know what kind of relationship they *don't* want with money. They've tasted that fear. Like me, they've seen fear etched on their parents' faces. People who've experienced poverty often have a greater drive and a stronger commitment to change. I know people like this. I admire them.

On the other hand, those raised in relative ease and comfort often have the hardest time changing their relationship to money. Sometimes, they've developed unrealistic expectations. In some cases, others have bailed them out for so long, they've never had to learn the true cost of living. They've never suffered the consequences of bad money management. They've never felt that bone-chilling fear of pending financial doom, the kind of fear that forces you to change. They've also never experienced the glory of turning things around and making them right again.

Here's the point: No matter what your 90-Day Number tells you about your current financial circumstances, you've had a good look at your internal financial wiring. And no matter what you learned, you now know there's room for improvement. It's entirely up to you to change. And you can.

Money Mistake: You're Drowning in Credit Card Debt

THE FIX: READ THE FINE PRINT

Spending too much is a disease. And credit card debt is a cancer. The first time you get a credit card bill and don't pay off the full balance, it's as if you've allowed the first financial cancer cell into your life. The compounding nature of those frightening interest rates is a monstrous thing to behold. Take a look at your credit card bill. Put on some reading glasses and peer at the dangerous fine print. By law, credit card companies are required to tell you how many years it will take to pay off your balance if you pay only the minimum each month. For instance, if you owe $5,000 and you make only a minimum payment of $100 a month at an interest rate of 19 percent, it will take you eight years and three months to pay that off. Now, get this: The average U.S. household is $34,000 in debt. And that's just consumer debt! That's not counting mortgages. The numbers are staggering but true: The average American family owes $27,000 in college loans and $7,000 in credit card debt. Most of these debtors are buying cars on credit, or paying for vacations or expensive home renovations.

The credit card companies will tell you their ridiculously high interest rates are necessary insurance against people who defraud them or default on their balances. But the truth is that they make most of their money off people who can't pay off their balances. It's that simple. The card companies have found their infinite supply of cash flow—generation after generation of overspenders. Think about the credit card company that occupies a world where its average return is 16 percent. Now *there's* a business that makes good money! Imagine if your investments paid you 16 percent, week after week, month after month, in perpetuity. How far would you go to protect that return? Pretty darn far, I bet. That's why credit is so easy to come by. These companies throw out a global net to see which suckers they can snag into that morass of debt. And many of you get caught willingly. But here's the problem: Once that 16 percent compounds, you're in trouble, because you can never, ever earn a 16 percent return consistently and fast enough on anything to offset the insidious growth of that kind of debt. You can't dig yourself out of that kind of hole. Nobody can.

Here's the kicker: There's nothing illegal about the credit industry. And it's so powerful that when any righteous politician introduces legislation to outlaw criminally exorbitant interest rates, and this happens at every election, the idea usually dies quickly and quietly in a series of discreet meetings where well-dressed lobbyists never have to speak louder than a whisper. Banks are the smartest corporate entities on the planet. That's why I invest in them.

The real tragedy, if not the real crime, of personal overspending is that any bartender is legally bound to cut off a dangerously drunk person. But you won't see that happening in a store. No cashiers at Neiman Marcus or Saks are going to place their hand over your credit card and suggest you don't really need three pairs of skinny jeans, that one pair will suffice. Nope. They'll congratulate you on your "finds" and reinforce the fact that you "deserve to splurge."

Money Mistake: You Use Your Partner's Credit Card

THE FIX: ESTABLISH YOUR OWN CREDIT RATING—FAST!

Credit cards are the primary culprit behind most compulsive spending and personal debt. But I'm not advocating that you avoid credit cards altogether. You need a credit rating of some kind, or you can't qualify for a mortgage and other financial products you may need. In other words, even though credit cards can be dangerous, it's worse if you *don't* have one. My wife experienced this dilemma firsthand. When we got married more than twenty years ago, we folded what little money we had together into one account. We had one checking account and one credit card, in my name, but we each carried a version of the card. For decades, we never really thought much about that division, until many years later, when Linda wanted to apply for a department store credit card. Despite our household income, she was declined. She hadn't, in all those years, established *any credit rating whatsoever,* which, we discovered, is almost as bad as having a poor rating. This is a frightening prospect, and it's a conundrum that traps a lot of women—especially widows, like the one I met in Beacon Hill, who had no idea whose name her credit cards were in. Had anything happened to me, Linda would have had a very tough time applying for a card to establish a credit history. It's an awful thing to learn at the funeral of your partner that you can't function financially. Without a credit rating, you can't borrow money or own property, your largest potential asset. Get wise, and establish a credit rating now.

We didn't make the same mistakes with our children. As soon as my daughter, Savannah, was old enough and living on her own, she applied for a credit card. I sat down with her and walked her through the small print that outlines how compound interest allows the bank to own her soul until she's solvent or dies. I also explained to her that she should have a separate no-fee, low-limit credit card for purchases online. Why do this? Internet fraud is insidious and hard to stanch. If an online thief gets hold of your secondary credit card number, at least the damage will be limited.

Money Mistake: You're in a Consumer Trance

THE FIX: SNAP OUT OF IT

Many people confuse my love of money with a love of "stuff." These two things could not be more different. I love money because, employed properly, it's a source of creative energy; "stuff," on the other hand, merely uses up energy by killing money. We buy stuff with money, and, more often than not, this stuff becomes a vessel for more spending. The car that requires gas and repairs; that too-big house that needs electricity and fuel to heat it; that walk-in closet you have to fill.

Here's how to break that trance. I want to look closely at the word *interest*. Every single time you purchase something on a credit card or a line of credit that you don't pay off immediately, you're paying interest. Ask yourself every time you choose to whip out that card and buy something: Will the interest I pay on this item outlive my interest *in* this item? If the answer is yes, don't buy it! Think of that attractive person you once dated years ago. Looking back now, it's easy to see you didn't actually need him or her. You don't need that person now, right? But imagine if, contractually, you were obligated to keep spending time with the very person you now feel absolutely nothing for, until he or she says it's over. Sounds insane, but many consumers are making exactly that bargain with things they purchase, things they said they loved and needed, yet days, weeks, and months later, they're bound to keep paying for something they no longer enjoy.

Here's another way to think about it: When you buy something you can't afford with money that's not yours, but a bank's, you're effectively stealing. The only reason we don't go to jail for this is that the institution from which you're stealing is insured against this theft. That's what interest is to a bank: a kind of insurance—that *you* pay for your thievery.

Here's the coldest, hardest truth about consumer spending: Every single thing about your beloved purchase diminishes after you throw it on a credit card—everything except the cost. They say the definition of insanity is doing the same thing over and over again and expecting a different result. What different result are we hoping for when we slap another thing we don't need on a credit card? That *this* time the feeling it creates will last? That *this* time its value will last the product's life span? That's not going to happen—ever. When you buy on credit, luster, newness, and novelty will diminish, but the price tag will always get bigger.

Money Mistake: Spending Makes You Happy

THE FIX: GET A HANDLE ON EMOTIONAL SPENDING

Men and women spend too much because it feels good, temporarily. It's not more complicated than that. But as I say over and over again, feelings and money are a toxic combination. If you're bored, lonely, frustrated, or sad, don't go shopping to change your mood. Do anything, in fact, *but* shop. Go for a walk, cook, read, but don't head for the mall.

It's not enough to stanch the flow of funds out; you need to understand why you spend, why you have a tendency to put yourself in precarious financial situations, over and over again—especially if overspending is affecting your health or your relationships. See a specialist in compulsive behavior. Check out a Debtors Anonymous meeting to see if it's for you. And find other pleasures, other pursuits beyond shopping and spending, that give you satisfaction, fulfillment, and joy. Most important, don't hang around other emotional spenders—friends who subtly pressure you to drop half your paycheck on those shoes that look so good on you. Spending can be a contagious disease. If you have a friend who is justifying and enabling your spending problem, at the very least don't shop with that person. And I like this classic bit of advice: Put your cards in containers, cover them with water, and throw them in the freezer. You won't damage the cards, and if you still want to make that purchase twenty-four hours after you let the cards thaw out, fine. But freezing your cards forces you to think it over before you buy. You may also want to limit your exposure to persuasive ads and red-hot deals that constantly assault the senses. So you might have to stop buying magazines, watching late-night TV, and mindlessly surfing the Internet at least for ninety days, until you have better control over your spending. Advertising is insidious, subliminal, and peripheral; ads are everywhere, so you can't completely cut off your exposure. But you can limit what comes into your house. So unsubscribe from those magazines, get offline more often, and don't forget to DVR your favorite TV shows. That way you can fast-forward through the commercials.

Money Mistake: Frugality Isn't Fun

THE FIX: CREATE A "FUN MONEY" FUND

If eliminating debt and saving money are priorities for you, then some measure of austerity has to be instituted. You do have to tighten your belt and keep a closer eye on your wallet. That's a given. But a certain kind of joylessness can also creep in. It happens with dieters who deprive themselves of anything fattening, decadent, or delicious in a punishing quest to reach their goal weight. You hear the stories of late-night binges triggered by weeks, months, even years of constant deprivation. That's not a way to live, and that's not what I'm advocating in these pages. Austerity, yes; deprivation, no. In fact, spending on fun things should be part of your budget. I suggest that you set aside a manageable percentage every week in a fund that will allow you to splurge with cash. Let yourself do whatever you want with that money. Buy something that gives you pleasure, go on a trip, get your hair done—as long as you pay for it outright. These are the kinds of shopping trips you get to fully and completely enjoy, guilt-free.

Cold Hard Truth Card

If you're serious about getting your finances in order, cut out this card from the book, front and back (sorry it leaves a nasty hole in your book, but it's worth it). Or better yet, write the card out in your own handwriting. KEEP THIS CARD IN YOUR PURSE OR WALLET. That's an order. Every time you are about to make a purchase—and I mean every time—for clothing, food, liquor, appliances, lipstick, concert tickets, or anything at all—first pull out this card. Read it to yourself. Before you pay for your goods, decide whether you are in a consumer trance or operating in good sense. If you're in a trance, put the goods down. Walk away from the store, close the laptop, or turn off the TV. Say— out loud—"I'm proud of myself. I've done the right thing. I've woken up from the trance. I've saved my money."

I pledge to make no purchases unless I can answer TRUE to the following FIVE statements.

1. I have given this purchase sufficient thought.
2. Buying this item will not create debt for me or anyone else.
3. I not only want this item, I need it.
4. This item is more valuable than the interest I'd earn if I saved the money instead.
5. This item will matter to me in a year.

Signature

KEVIN O'LEARY, INC.

COLD HARD TRUTH CARD

I pledge to make no purchases unless I can answer TRUE to the following FIVE statements.

1. I have given this purchase sufficient thought.
2. Buying this item will not create debt for me or anyone else.
3. I not only want this item, I need it.
4. This item is more valuable than the interest I'd earn if I saved the money instead.
5. This item will matter to me in a year.

Signature _____

(Random House Canada/Kathryn Hollinrake)

CHAPTER 3

Save Your Money, Save Your Life

People who are good with money, as my mother was, know how to say no. But mostly, they know how to live within their means. I define that as living just below what you can afford so that you always have extra. That extra gap is what is saved. That's the idea I want you to wrap your head around. People who live within—or even better, *below*—their means are good with money. And they *enjoy* the feeling of plenty around them. They get used to that feeling, so being financially overextended creates physical unease. And it's a true physical phenomenon. The stress of debt and financial hardship takes a serious toll on our health, on our relationships, and on our ability to earn the money we need to get out of that hole. A few years ago, an Associated Press–AOL Health poll found a link between money problems and a high rate of ulcers, migraines, Type 2 diabetes, and heart disease. People under stress also tend to smoke and drink more and sleep a lot less. So you see the catch-22. Financial health and personal health are deeply related.

Kevin O'Leary

The 90-Day Number is a way for you to diagnose that problem and get a handle on the health of your cash flow. It's also a way to break that consumer trance and begin stanching the flow of money out. Now we're going to channel some of the excess into a savings account, which for some people is even harder to do than investing, and it's certainly not as fun as spending.

So here's my challenge to those of you who don't think you can save money: Try saving a set amount of money for *only three months*. Don't think of it as a lifetime adjustment. Consider it temporary discomfort, like a cast around a broken ankle, a cast that's going to come off soon. Start with just $100 a month, if you can, or less, if that's too much. What's the worst thing that can happen? You'll have $300 at the end of the experiment. That's the obvious outcome, but the result you want to achieve is the mild discomfort you'll feel in month four, when you don't set aside your $100. As I said earlier, people who are good with money don't feel well when they're overextended. Instead of avoiding that kind of discomfort, cultivate it.

Money Mistake: You Have No Emergency Savings

THE FIX: SET ASIDE SOMETHING—ANYTHING

We can't talk about saving and investing and other financial vehicles until you get a handle on your output. I want you to be able to walk past those shoes, that boat, that car—even that cup of coffee—and be able to say no. Because you'll have created a comfortable financial threshold you can live just beneath. This is, after all, a health issue—your and your family's health.

38

Let's put a number on it. This gap between what you have and what you can afford should feel tangible. Going back to your 90-Day Number, and assuming you're now taking in less than you're putting out, the first thing to ask yourself is: *What is fixed and what is flexible about these numbers?* Let's assume your input is fixed, that the amount you take in isn't going to fluctuate in those ninety days. Using common metrics and basic math, let's also apply a few basic tenets of financial planning. Say your input is $4,000 after taxes. I'm rounding it up and down a little in each category to keep the numbers simple. This is also assuming there is a little debt, but nothing unmanageable. Again, we're looking at an ideal financial situation.

OUTPUT	PERCENTAGE OF INCOME	TOTALS IN $ SPENT
Housing	25%	1,000
Saving	5%	200
Investing	5%	200
Utilities	5%	200
Cable/Internet/Phone	5%	200
Food	10%	400
Transportation	10%	400
Recreation	5%	200
Debt	5%	200
Clothing	5%	200
Medical/Health/Gym	5%	200
Insurance	5%	200
Subtotal	**90%**	**3,600**
Cushion	10%	400
Total	**100%**	**4,000**

Again, these are estimates and options for spending that will vary. Maybe your housing cost is much higher, and you don't spend that much on clothing. Maybe you're servicing a bit more debt, or not servicing any. Regardless of how your income is specifically distributed, what I want you to notice is the 10 percent cushion under the subtotal. Remember that the cushion is on top of the 10 percent you invest and save, by the way. You're saving, investing, *and* putting away that cushion—because your goal is to live on 10 percent less than you normally do, even after you've factored in money set aside for savings and investing.

That's asking a lot. But I'm painting the ideal scenario. And I'm allowing for you to set aside money for the most important and often-ignored fund: your Catastrophe Cash Fund.

At first, that 10 percent will become your Catastrophe Cash Fund. When it reaches the amount you decided to set aside (say your total expenses for six months are $18,000), stop putting that money toward your Catastrophe Cash and start funneling that cushion back into your investments. To continue to live within your means, that's how you'll ease that percentage up ever so slightly, from 10 percent to 12 to 15, so that by the time you retire, you're already well adjusted to your new expectations, your new means, below which you will continue to live in relative financial bliss. If you're on a fixed income in retirement, whether you start tapping into your 401(k), pension, or annuity, you'll already be mentally and financially adjusted to your new reality. You're well on your way to enjoying life with a predictable amount of money flowing in, minus the low-level panic financial uncertainty breeds. Living within your means will feel natural. That's how to reach financial freedom—now.

This is a financial blueprint that suits most profiles, regardless of what income you're bringing in. It's not impossible, but it's tough. But here is the ultimate trick to building wealth and retiring in comfort and ease. It goes beyond just living within your means. You must stay within your means. As you earn more income, remain exactly where you're at. In other words, *with every exponential increase in your salary, don't match it with lifestyle spending.* Treat your increased earnings as a bonus, not a given, and certainly not as a prompt to stretch beyond your boundaries. Shave off a nice percentage that you can splurge with, but sock the rest of the money away, or pay down your mortgage. Don't get caught in the loop of living larger and larger just because you think you can. Here's one thing I know about really wealthy people: They find that set point of "enough" and then they rarely exceed it. Once they find that set point, they don't spend more extravagantly as their income increases. They bank and invest that extra money, but continue to enjoy life at the level of luxury they already defined as "enough." That extra cushion of cash provides them with enough security to weather any storm. This is something everyone should do, and that everyone *can* do, regardless of how much they have.

Money Mistake: You Don't Know How Much Money You Waste

THE FIX: CALCULATE (AND SAVE) YOUR GHOST MONEY

I love compound-interest charts almost as much as I love compound interest. There's no more tangible way to see money grow. Those charts are also a chilling way to watch money die. Ghost Money is dead money, money wasted on stupid things, money that should have been invested instead. Let's put a cost on that kind of wasted money, and learn new ways to save a fortune for your retirement.

The average American regularly spends money automatically, unconsciously, on four common purchases: coffee, magazines, lunches, and alcohol. What I'm going to show you is how casually money is flushed down the toilet. And what a $3-a-day Starbucks coffee could have been instead.

Let's start conservatively with some typical unconscious spending habits. Say you buy two magazines a month ($10), you purchase coffee twice a week ($6), you buy lunch once a week ($10), and you go out for a couple of happy hour drinks on Fridays ($10), because you call yourself a "social drinker."

Now, let's look at the approximate cost of these purchases over ten years—if the cost never goes up—with 4 percent compounded interest.

		SUBTOTAL (Compounded)	WITH 4% INTEREST (Rounded Off)	TOTAL
Coffee	$6/week for 10 years	3,120	800	3,920
Magazines	$10/month for 10 years	1,200	300	1,500
Lunch	$10/week for 10 years	5,200	1,300	6,500
Alcohol	$10/week for 10 years	5,200	1,300	6,500
Grand Total		**14,720**	**3,700**	**18,420**

Ten years of unconscious spending on just those four items killed $18,420—money that should have been invested, which even at a conservative interest rate would have generated a small fortune. I look at that total and actually feel sad about the loss. Ghost Money is a sad thing. If this looks familiar to you and you can see in this your own poor spending habits, I hope the loss is haunting you. It should be. But maybe $18,420 isn't a significant enough figure to scare you awake. The example above illustrated unconscious purchases of a very moderate spender.

Now let's take out that financial Ouija board and call up some real bloodcurdling Ghost Money created by a really big unconscious spender over the course of twenty years—someone who complains he never has enough money at the end of the month, yet there he is, lining up for his fancy coffee four times a week, saying he's too busy to make his own lunch and take it to work. Oh, and now he drinks a couple of beers every night, because "social drinking" moved from the restaurant bar to the living room sofa a long time ago. He commutes by public transit, but he buys a lot of glossy magazines off the rack for something to read every day. Not only does he spend constantly and unconsciously, he spends like this for *decades*. This is his approximate Ghost Money over twenty years of habitual, incidental, noncrucial spending, with compounded interest set at a more realistic 6 percent—which, in fact, has been the forty-year interest rate average. (This also assumes the base price never goes up, and we all know that's not the case with alcohol.)

		SUBTOTAL	6% INTEREST (Rounded Off)	TOTAL
Coffee	$12/week for 20 years	12,480	11,820	24,300
Magazines	$8/week for 20 years	8,320	7,900	16,220
Lunch	$200/month for 20 years	48,000	45,600	93,600
Alcohol	$10/day for 20 years	73,000	69,300	142,300
Grand Total		**141,800**	**134,620**	**276,420**

So what does our big unconscious spender have to show for all these purchases? A grand total of $276,420 in Ghost Money. Gone. Instead of putting that money into an account that accrued interest, this person bought *People* every week. Instead of saving for retirement, he enjoyed half-caf mochaccinos many mornings. Big money rarely dies suddenly. It's usually slowly drained away over long periods of time, bit by bit, penny by penny, so slowly that it's hardly noticeable. It's as if that money never existed to begin with. In other words, it doesn't haunt you. But what if you took that amount of money, organized it into a neat pile in your backyard, and set fire to it? Wouldn't that traumatize you? I bet it would. I want you to start being haunted by Ghost Money, to feel its loss when you spend on unnecessary items. I want this lost money to stand by your bed at night, like Marley over Ebenezer Scrooge, and shake its chains at your financial folly.

How do you bring that kind of Ghost Money back to life? How do you leave behind the suckers who line up for their expensive coffees and magazines and spend their money on a bad habit that will likely kill them? The good news is that it's not too late. Some of that Ghost Money *can* come back to life, if you introduce savvy spending habits now. Because I'll tell you something else about Ghost Money: If it doesn't haunt you now, it'll haunt you later. I believe in Money Karma. This is how it works: If you spend a wad of cash on cappuccinos and magazines in your twenties, there's a good chance you'll be serving coffee or working at a newsstand in your seventies to pay for your retirement. Remember that there is a certain amount of money you need to earn to take care of yourself during your lifetime, and you're going to have to earn it somehow. If you don't want to get a job at Starbucks in your twilight years, stop spending so much money there today. Money knows when it's being wasted.

It remembers when it's been disrespected, so keep that karma in mind when you're lining up for your morning fix.

Money Mistake: Friends and Family Ask You for Money

THE FIX: DON'T LEND, GIVE (IF YOU CAN)

There is no greater minefield, no bigger potential for disastrous rifts, than when family lends money to family. So I am often baffled when I get flak on *Shark Tank* for saying money and tears don't mix. In all my years on TV, no one's ever asked me why that's so. I'll tell you now. It's because emotions aren't factual. You can't accurately measure them, and they change constantly. Money, on the other hand, is factual—you can measure it. Money doesn't change. Therefore, I see money and emotions as incompatible forces. Like oil and water, they don't mix. Think of the toxic results of emotional spending. Think of how wrenching it is when a member of your family begs you for money you know you'll never see again. Lending friends and family money is one of the worst forms of Ghost Money there is because it breeds real resentment—which, by definition, is a feeling that is felt over and over again. Every time you see that person to whom you've lent money, feelings of anger and regret will creep in. What a way to ruin a relationship.

That's why you must have the discipline to say no to lending money you're not prepared to give. Start by separating yourself emotionally from your own money, or you'll be plagued by people trying to part you and your cash. *You must begin to think of your money as the very blood that runs through your body. It's that vital.* Money is a life force, like blood. You need a certain amount or you'll die. You can live after a severe loss of blood, but you won't feel well until you're replenished. Thinking this way has made me very selective when it comes to parting with my money. That's why I have no problem saying no to people who try to appeal to my emotions.

Next time your brother comes to you with a personal plea to invest your $30,000 in his restaurant, say no on behalf of your money. When your child is throwing a temper tantrum in the aisle of the grocery story until you buy his or her favorite snack, you must say no on behalf of your money. If your husband makes a counteroffer after you kiboshed his golf trip in order to pay off some debt, you must say no on behalf of your money.

Lending people money so they don't get mad at you is as bad as compulsive spending. And once begun, lending money, like compulsive spending, is a very dangerous habit to break. I'm no psychotherapist, but I do know this: Compulsive spending and lending don't end anywhere good. They have to stop.

I offer this caveat, however: There's another way to handle these requests. *Give* your brother the money. But give only an amount you're comfortable *never seeing again*. That's right: Even if your brother insists it's a loan, treat it like a gift. Never expect to see money you loan friends or family again, and it will divorce emotion from that transaction and preempt any toxic resentment that may result if your brother doesn't pay you back. Best news is, you never have to do this again. Next time your brother asks, tell him you already gave him money. That was very generous and will suffice.

Reviving Ghost Money

Earlier in the book, I asked you to calculate your 90-Day Number. Now I'm going to ask you to go to my website, www .kevinoleary.com, and find the Ghost Money calculator. The calculator is a tool that will show you how much Ghost Money your unconscious spending and lending have created, with the added bonus of the compounded interest that the money would have earned had it been properly deployed as an investment. Put in the items you've regularly spent money on in the last five to ten years, or however long you've been problematically, automatically spending on incidentals. Be honest and realistic. What you'll be calculating is your own Ghost Money fund, and figuring out how much you can resuscitate now, with just a few adjustments to your incidental spending habits. Here are a few ideas to stanch the flow of your Ghost Money.

1. **Magazines.** Never buy them off the rack. Rack prices are inflated, so it's the most expensive way to get your fix. Always subscribe, or get a tablet and download them. Local libraries let you read them for free. And if you work in an industry where it's important to stay abreast of news and current affairs, convince your boss to buy the magazines for you. Besides, chopping trees down for magazines and newspapers is going to become an obsolete practice. We live in an increasingly wireless, paperless world. Embrace it.

2. **Alcohol.** There's no kind way to say this: If you're drinking every night, you're an idiot. I was once an idiot, too, by the way. Relaxing over an occasional cocktail is one thing; drinking like there's no tomorrow is another. Frequent

alcohol use has an excellent track record of burning holes in wallets. Have you been to a bar lately? Even five bucks is way too much for a beer, and don't even get me started on $14 "signature cocktails." I can't justify paying that much to slowly kill myself, and neither should you. You've just carved a path from your wallet directly into the alcohol companies' bank accounts. If you refuse to quit, you should be saving an equivalent of what you spend on alcohol into your Catastrophe Cash account. You're going to need it when you get cirrhosis and can no longer work and your children haven't saved enough to bury you properly. Sorry to be grim, but you know it's true. If you really think you have a problem, get help as soon as possible. Lighten up on the booze and your money will thank you. So will your liver.

3. **Coffee/Lunches.** Speaking of moronic, it never fails to amaze me when I see young interns and assistants paying $25 a day on fancy coffees and lunches, when I know it took them the better part of the morning to earn it. So I can't stress this enough: Take the time and put in the effort to make your own coffee and lunches at home! Invest in a thermos, a vinyl lunch bag, and a good coffee maker. Because I'm not exaggerating when I say this: Lunch and coffee spending are the kind of insidious, daily expenditures that erode wealth and can affect your quality of life down the road.

————

There is always a cheaper way to enjoy your life, one that won't take away any of the pleasures and won't create more financial pain down the line. In fact, being frugal increases your sense of economic security and overall quality of life. That's the only way to experience the kind of joy only truly financially stable people get to feel. You can take this a step further. After becoming keenly aware of the Ghost Money you're creating and pledging to stop creating more, put that money you saved back into a Ghost Money fund. A year of no longer grabbing a couple of beers after work could add up to almost $4,000. Change is so much easier to institute when you can see the results.

CHAPTER 4

Invest Right, Invest Now

Every relationship you have is an investment. Take a look at them. How many of those relationships actually "pay off"? How many pay dividends commensurate to the amount of time and effort you put into them? I'm talking about emotional dividends. That's how you measure the health of each relationship. The ones that don't pay off tend to get less of your attention over time, to the point where they eventually fade away. And it's a two-way street. If you don't give, you don't get—the dividends of any relationship reflect that. Money works the same way. Disregard it, ignore it, don't take pains to protect it, and your money will disappear. Conversely, if you do your part in your "money relationships," money will reciprocate. I promise you.

What's your part? You are the saver, the spender, and the savvy investor in this relationship. You are the steward of your money. I discussed why it's important to get a clear snapshot of your 90-Day Number, because it teaches you about your current relationship with money. I also showed you how to break that consumer trance so you can avoid Ghost Money and keep it all real, in your wallet and in savings or accounts. You'll begin to free up money you already have so you can start investing, as often and as early as possible. It doesn't matter how much you invest. What matters is that you start—and soon.

Money Mistake: You Don't Know When to Start Investing

THE FIX: START WHEN YOU'RE DEBT-FREE

Ideally, you'll start investing as soon as possible and steadily ever after. Most people who have compound-interest charts tattooed inside their eyelids are not shocked to learn that $10,000 invested in their twenties will be worth $58,000 at age sixty-five, assuming a 4 percent compounded interest rate. What's shocking is that so many young people don't take advantage of that. But how many twenty-three-year-olds are truly in a position to put away that kind of money? Not many. So here's a simple rule: Start investing when you're free of consumer debt. No matter what age that is, when you're no longer servicing a student loan, or paying down credit cards, or making car payments, start investing your money. How much? Start with the amount you used to funnel toward that debt. The trick is not to incur any more consumer debt so that the flow of funds into your investments isn't interrupted once you make that commitment. No matter how old you are, the day you start investing is the day you've decided to take control of your future. I don't care if this happens when you're fifty-two years old.

Money Mistake: You Don't Know What to Invest In

THE FIX: KEEP IT SIMPLE

The first question is simple: Should I invest in stocks, mutual funds, or bonds? The answer is also simple: yes. The specifics vary from person to person, but the core of my own investment philosophy stemmed from watching my mother grow her own considerable nest egg with a consistent amount of money, very little effort, and a lot of discipline. She had three basic rules:

1. Never invest in a security or stock that doesn't pay a dividend or interest.
2. Always save a consistent portion of your income.
3. Spend the interest, never the principal.

My mother hammered this home to me every payday, so much so that these became the core principles upon which I built O'Leary Funds. Why did she invest like this? Back in the fifties, investors wanted to get paid for their risk. They wanted, say, a 7 percent dividend on their IBM stock in case the company nosedived. They wanted a little something, some goodwill, in return for trusting the company not to put their hard-earned money in harm's way. They were conservative investors, the kind who would *never* sink a dime into a non-dividend-paying stock like Dell or Google—or Facebook, for that matter, a company that's impossible to value accurately because it doesn't return any cash to its shareholders. Quite simply, dividends are barometers of a company's worth and health. My mother would have watched Facebook's IPO the way other people watch horror movies. All those people! All that money! And for what, exactly?

In the mid-2000s, I was a broad and avid investor. I had made a fortune when I sold The Learning Company to Mattel in 1998, a deal that netted me, my partners, and our shareholders $4.2 billion. I was living in Boston at the time and put half my earnings with my money managers. The other half I invested heavily in hedge funds based in Boston and New York. Eventually, I found myself sinking two-thirds of my money into hedge funds. This was very uncharacteristic of me, focusing such a big portion of my portfolio in one sector, but the high returns were too good to resist.

Then came the financial crisis. In 2008, the hedge fund sector collapsed in an illiquidity trap. Hedge fund managers gated their fund flows, restricting the amount of withdrawals investors could make. A gate provision is almost always a negative event, and for good reason: The values of hedge funds plummeted almost overnight. So I lost a significant chunk of my equity. All I could do was sit idly by and watch.

I experienced a massive gut check, and a harsh lesson. What was I thinking? I was not that kind of investor. I was not the kind of guy who puts two-thirds of his portfolio in any one sector or asset class. I got caught up, and I got caught out. As I mentioned, around this time my mother passed away, and, as executor of her estate, I saw how steadily investing in stocks or securities that paid a dividend or a yield only grew steadily over time. Here's why my own mother's portfolio outperformed everything.

As you can see from this chart, over a forty-year period, more than 70 percent of the total returns on the stock market came from investments that yielded dividends, not from those that relied on capital appreciation. In other words, people like my mother who invested in stocks that paid you something did

O'LEARY FUNDS   Yield Dominates Long–Term Total Return

Prioritize Yield Rather Than Depend on Growth
"Get Paid While You Wait"®

(Bloomberg)

better than those who invested only in hopes that the companies themselves would increase in value. This was mind-blowing to me. The day I saw my mother's portfolio was the day I stopped buying stocks that didn't pay anything to shareholders. Overnight, this became the only way I wanted to invest. But trying to find money managers who agreed with me, who would follow this mandate strictly, proved to be very difficult—until I met a man with a similar vision: Connor O'Brien. Together we formed O'Leary Funds, which is a family of financial products now worth more than $1 billion. Our philosophy is "Get Paid While You Wait," which is exactly what my mother did. Except for gold, O'Leary Funds deals only in dividend-paying stocks and interest-bearing bonds. As a result, we have tremendous focus. If it doesn't pay, we don't play.

At some point, I have to believe my mother would have asked herself these questions:

- Who is paying you to wait?
- What is this company giving you in exchange for holding on to your money?

They have to give you something. It's that simple. That's where you start when you think about investing: Ask yourself what's in it for you to give that company your money.

Let me put it this way: When you invest in a stock that doesn't pay a dividend, you're effectively saying to the CEO of that company or its board of directors, "Here. Here's my money. You keep *my portion* of those profits that my money's helping you generate and you redeploy it because you know what's best for this company. Buy a new plant, retire debt, expand into a different country, or create a new product—you decide." That's what investors must have thought to themselves when they bought popular stocks such as Dell or Yahoo.

As you can see, these non-dividend-paying stocks did not perform well. Worse, you'll never really know what went wrong with that company, so you're never going to find out exactly what happened to your money.

Here's what I believe, and why investing in companies that pay dividends is the best option. The culture of companies mandated to pay you a dividend is different from that of those whose mandate it is to simply grow market share and create profit. I believe a CEO of a company that's paying me a dividend wakes up every morning and says, "Today I have to make sure my expenses are in line and my profits and cash flow are adequate to pay Mr. O'Leary his dividend."

O'LEARY FUNDS

Investing in Dividend Paying Equities

Dividend Equities have a Strong Performance History

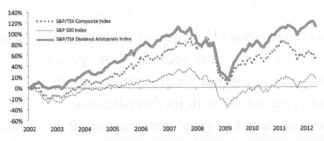

	2002	2003	2004	2005	2006	2007	2008	2009	2010	2011	2012 YTD	Annualized 2002-2012*	Index Yield 07/04/2012
S&P/TSX Composite Index	-14%	24%	12%	22%	15%	7%	-35%	31%	14%	-11%	-3%	5.0%	3.0%
S&P 500 Index	-23%	26%	9%	3%	14%	4%	-38%	23%	13%	0%	8%	3.2%	2.1%
S&P/TSX Dividend Aristocrat Index	2%	21%	16%	20%	14%	0%	-36%	45%	12%	4%	0%	7.0%	4.1%

Source: Stanton Asset Management Inc.; Bloomberg. Chart data as at June, 2012. *June 2002-June 2012.

This presentation is confidential and for advisor use only.
The contents are not to be reproduced or distributed to the public or press.
This page is not complete without the disclaimers from page 2.

(Bloomberg)

16

CEOs of companies that don't pay a dividend aren't thinking about the shareholder as a top priority. They're thinking about themselves. They're thinking about their profits, their benefits. When that's the case, I don't invest. This is controversial, advising people to dump stocks that aren't paying them a dividend, even healthy ones, but numbers—and history—don't lie.

Money Mistake: You Don't Invest Because You Don't Know How

THE FIX: INVEST LIKE A WOMAN

Want more controversy? Here goes: I believe women make better investors than men. I am speaking from personal evidence, as someone who has seen a lot of investment portfolios. When a portfolio impresses me with its diversification, its risk profile, and its commitment to capital preservation, it has invariably been owned by a woman. Now, why is that? I believe it stems from the notion that historically, at least, a woman's finances have always been more precarious than a man's. Hence, it seems that some women value security more and therefore take fewer risks when it comes to managing their investments. Also, women who are the primary caregivers of the family don't invest thinking only of themselves. They tend to invest more broadly, and more conservatively.

Here is my own investment rule of thumb: *Never invest more than 5 percent into any one stock and never more than 20 percent into any one sector.* Time and again, when I see a portfolio with 80 percent of someone's money invested in one sector, it is a man who's assuming this kind of risk.

My mother protected her principal at all costs. If she put capital at risk, she needed to be paid to do that in the form of dividends or interest. Maybe the reason I had always resisted that kind of investing was that there seemed to be something almost stereotypically feminine about it, not "risky" or "driven."

My tune has changed dramatically.

I talked about getting to a point in life where you are no longer paying anything—anything but taxes. This is how you start to tip the balance back in your favor. As an investor, quite simply, you must get paid something for that risk. The sooner in life you start investing, the sooner you can tip that scale away from paying interest on loans and mortgages, and start getting paid for waiting it out with your money deployed. There are exceptions. Gold, for instance. I do own gold in my portfolio. In fact, 5 percent of my portfolio is composed of this security. It does not pay a dividend, but I like to think that it provides stability. Every ninety days or so, I buy or sell my gold to keep its share of the portfolio at 5 percent.

Kevin O'Leary's Personal Investment Portfolio

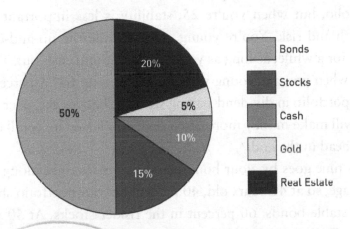

*Bonds are tricky. Bottom line is you have to own the right bonds at the right time. These days, I don't own sovereign debt or government bonds because their interest rates are at all-time lows. Governments are proving over and over that they have a difficult time running things. Not so with corporations (which is why capitalism works!). In my portfolio, you'll find only bonds comprising corporate debt—those with an average duration of less than five years. However, when it comes to buying bonds, I strongly advise you to find a good financial advisor to help you.

Money Mistake: You Invest the Same Way All Through Life

THE FIX: MATCH YOUR INVESTMENT RATIO TO YOUR AGE

Here is a simple way to keep an eye on your investments and make simple adjustments to it as you age. To explain this model, let's keep the numbers and ratios simple. Let's say you start investing when you're 25 years old. Let's also assume you're going to live to be 85 years old. With this scenario, you have 40 years to grow your money to age of 65, after which point you'll retire. That means you'll need your money to last you for 20 years.

In this scenario, at 25 years of age, 25 percent of your portfolio should be in secure, predictable bonds. Bonds stabilize your portfolio, but when you're 25, stability is less important than growth and risk. You're young, you can ride the up-and-down wave for a while, as long as you don't panic and cash out. Therefore, when you are young you should have up to 75 percent of your portfolio in dividend-paying stocks. Chances are, over time, you will make money more often than you'll lose it. You'll come out ahead in the end.

As time goes by, your bond percentage rises right along with your age, so at 40 years old, 40 percent of your portfolio should be in stable bonds, 60 percent in the riskier stocks. At 50 years old, half of your portfolio will be dividend-paying stocks, half in bonds. Easy to remember 50/50 at 50. After age 65, you need to start extracting the risk from your portfolio, so by the time you're 70, your portfolio is mostly bonds, and only 30 percent in riskier dividend-collecting stocks.

Learning to save well, spend smartly, and invest wisely signals the beginning of a fascinating and rewarding journey. Arm yourself with knowledge, understand your own appetite for risk, and be willing to ask for help. Follow that last bit of advice and you'll do fine.

You've picked up this book because you know I know money. I helm a mutual fund company with my name on it. But I am also here to tell you there is no guru who gets it right all the time, not even the venerable Warren Buffett, though the man comes close. Don't get sucked in by some weekend seminar that hypes you up on a sector or investment "method" that is a "tried and true" formula, "proven," and "guaranteed." There are no such things when it comes to investing.

Money Mistake: You Invested in Real Estate

THE FIX: GO TO WAR ON YOUR MORTGAGE FIRST

I once met an elderly man from Minneapolis. It was after a talk I gave about O'Leary Funds. He was from an Eastern European country that had shifted borders so many times during World War II that the country he was born in has a different name today. He was wearing a pair of dusty pants, a hat, and suspenders. We got to talking about investing in stocks and bonds, and he shook his head and held up his hand. He told me he invested only in property. That was it. I winced. I like to see diversification in a portfolio, especially when someone is investing later in life. But a few more minutes of chatting and it soon became apparent that this old, unkempt man owned huge swaths of residential and commercial real estate! This is a man who fled fascists as a child, who arrived in the United States with a fistful of papers and a few coins, who couldn't speak English, and who today is a multimillionaire. It blew my mind.

"How did you do it?" I asked.

"I went to war every day."

"War? Against what?"

"My mortgage," he said, with a twinkle in his eye.

Real estate is a tricky investment. I don't recommend that real estate compose more than 20 percent of any investment portfolio, but people's homes often constitute as much as 80 percent of their portfolio. It's their one big investment, which they plan to liquidate for their retirement. But too many people make the same mistake when calculating the true value of their investments. They total the market price of the property they own and call that their worth. But it's not. If you live in a $300,000 home and have only $60,000 of it in equity, you don't own $300,000 worth of real estate. You own $60,000. The bank owns the rest. In fact, you're worth less, because to liquidate that asset, you'll lose another 12 to 15 percent in fees, to your lawyer, your real estate agent, the land transfer tax, and those two guys hauling boxes. Don't even get me started on what you're going to get dinged in taxes.

But here was this older man in front of me, and he was clearly someone who understood real estate *as an investment.* He understood the only way it really works as an investment is if there is *no mortgage on that investment.* Any other scenario has the bank making money right along with you, usually more than you are making.

I couldn't help myself. I had to get his story. Here's what he told me. The first building he bought, in the mid-1950s, was a three-story walk-up with six units. It was in a bad neighborhood, so it was a risky but cheap investment. He had saved money while working at a restaurant and after five years was able to make a minimum 10 percent down payment. Then he was smart enough to strike a hard bargain with the bank. In exchange for buying and fixing up this decrepit building, he wanted the flexibility to pay down as much principal as possible every quarter. The bank, thinking this man would never be able to tackle that much of the mortgage that quickly, agreed. For the next five years, this man went to war, all day, every day, against his mortgage. It required a complete overhaul of his life.

"We ate beans," he said. "Lots of them. No meat. Beans. For years."

He burst out laughing as though this had been the best time in his life! He lived in the worst rental unit in the building he owned. Every dime he earned, he saved; every dollar of rent he collected that wasn't servicing the mortgage went into a separate savings account. Every three months, that tidy sum paid down the mortgage principal. He didn't rest and quit working; he didn't move to a bigger rental unit; he didn't spend any of his extra money on himself, his wife, or his kids until that mortgage no longer existed. And when it was all paid down in six, instead of twenty-six, years, he bought himself . . . a steak.

By then, of course, the previously decrepit building was in good condition and was generating a ton of rental income. So after eating his steak, what did he do with all the money he was earning? He saved it for a few months, and then put it toward a down payment on *another building*. He used the cash flow from the first building to service the mortgage on the second, and so on and so on, *for twenty years*. That's how he came to own half a city. That's how he became a multimillionaire in one generation.

But what's his true secret? Market timing? Good money management? A knack for finding good tenants and real estate gems? Sure. He was smart about all those things. But I think his real secret was this: *beans now, steak later.* If you have a mortgage, you have debt, and when you have debt, you don't get to have steak. The steak comes later. It's your reward. *That's* the kind of man I admire. I love how he became incredibly rich through diligence. I love how he used the bank's rules to his advantage and beat them at their own game.

His path to fortune was via residential property, but he shares the two traits that most wealthy people possess: a joyful frugality balanced by a painful aversion to debt. I want you to cultivate those two traits. Instead of being resentful that you can afford only beans because you've decided to cut spending, save aggressively and invest strategically. Let that sacrifice fill you with boundless pride. Because you're on the road to riches.

5 Investment Rules to Live By

Investing doesn't have to be scary or complicated. Here are five easy-to-follow investment rules that anyone can follow:

1. **Diversify.** Look at your portfolio and remember my rule. Make sure that you're investing only 5 percent of your money in any one stock or bond, and only 20 percent in any one segment (for example, energy). Anything more than that and you're courting risk and destabilizing your portfolio.
2. **Insist on dividends.** Never buy a security that doesn't pay a dividend or a bond that doesn't yield interest. Think of it like you're renting out your money. Don't let someone live in your spare room for free.
3. **Don't invest in anything you don't understand.** Billionaire Warren Buffett always abides by this rule. He puts his

money in *things,* not concepts. Oil, soap, insurance, computer technologies—these are recognizable products. He keeps it simple. When people invest in new products like "mortgage-backed securities" (which contributed to Wall Street's collapse), complicated derivatives (which kept regulators baffled), or high-tech start-ups (which sometimes generate ideas rather than products), they can get themselves in trouble. Skip them unless you know these products inside and out. Also, understand the tax implications of all your investments. Yes, you get a tax credit when you invest in a traditional IRA, but you pay taxes when you withdraw money from it, a detail many people leave out when they calculate their future income. That's why a good financial advisor is key to growing your wealth. A broker might help you pick your financial products, but an advisor will help you navigate the financial terrain.

4. **Don't be greedy.** It's called "B&H"—buy and hold. That means you don't want to buy and sell stocks with every single up and down of the market—a paranoid and insecure way to invest, and one that rarely leads to great success. Plus, it'll make you crazy, unless you're an experienced day trader.

5. **Don't believe the hype.** Stock tips are often a bunch of hokum designed to sell a product. It's all marketing. Trust your gut, and your money manager. Data can be interpreted a lot of ways, and a good broker knows how to understand the numbers. Go back to your mother's advice: If it's too good to be true, it is.

CHAPTER 5

Debt-Free First

It was a chilly Saturday morning in April. While everyone else was sleeping in, I got ready to meet a group of men and women who regularly gather near downtown Los Angeles to talk frankly and openly about how they got into so much trouble with money. They're members of something called Debtors Anonymous, an offshoot of Alcoholics Anonymous, except their addiction isn't to alcohol, but to creating enormous, crippling personal debt. I was invited to attend an open meeting where a member of the group was asked to share his story about the compulsive spending that landed him in the rooms of DA.

Maybe you're wondering why I would spend time in Debtors Anonymous when it's clear that my financial house is in fine order. Here's why: I wanted to see worst-case scenarios. I wanted to find out how people who've hit financial rock bottom can also turn things around. Most of us never let things get that bad, but we can all learn a lot from the people who've experienced the dark side of debt and overspending. Some addiction experts say overspending is a disease. And like a disease, if it progresses without being addressed, it's something that only gets worse over time. When you study the economy as I do, and understand the frightening level of household debt in North America, it's hard not to agree with the addiction experts. Still, looking around this bright room on the third floor of a beautifully restored building, I saw a few broke—and broken—men and women who'd made the worst mistakes you can with money. They went into debt to buy consumer goods; they never kept budgets; they were suckers for infomercials and impulse purchases at checkout counters; they bought lottery tickets and got seduced by get-rich-quick schemes; they bought clothes they never wore; they made big purchases without getting proper advice or thinking things through; they shopped emotionally to alleviate boredom, worry, anxiety, unhappiness, or a host of other unpleasant feelings; they spent money before it came in; they bought things for other people as a way to strengthen relationships or form intimacies; they hid, rationalized, and lied about their purchases to loved ones and others; they bought things they didn't need, leaving them with little left over for the things they *did* need, and all the while they felt increasingly sick and terrified as a result of their behavior. Meanwhile, their jobs and relationships suffered, and suddenly they found themselves broke, often jobless, and completely alone.

You won't find these faces on those joyous retirement posters in your bank, feet off the dock, enjoying their twilight years in relative ease and grace. And here's the thing: These people I met are suffering, no question, but society—that's us—is suffering along with them. Because their debts will become our debts. The illnesses they'll incur because of the stress they're facing will be our bills, in the form of increased taxes. When I say we're in this together, I'm not talking about holding hands and singing "Kumbaya" around the campfire. The stories I'm about to tell you are all true, and I'm telling them to you because I want you to be chilled to the bone. Think of me like a prison guard scaring you straight about your financial health. You don't want to be a member of Debtors Anonymous. Trust me on that. And no matter what stage of life you're at now, if you keep spending more than you make, this is where you'll end up.

A few of the attendees stared at the floor, full of shame and worry. Many were nicely put together, and at least on the surface it seemed their worst days were behind them. In fact, the room was filled with some of the best-dressed addicts I've ever seen! I guess that makes sense, considering that many of them got there because of bad shopping habits.

The speaker that day was a likeable guy named Paul. To look at him in his casual jeans and short-sleeved checked shirt, you wouldn't believe that he once owned a large, successful marketing company. But overspending and chronic credit card use eventually landed Paul half a million dollars in debt, with the government forcing him into bankruptcy. By the end of his spending and debt spree, his marriage was over, creditors were calling day and night, and he was practically homeless. After he spent the night on his brother's couch, his brother suggested Paul go to Debtors Anonymous to get some help. Left with no other option, he very reluctantly attended his first meeting. There, he slowly began to turn things around. Paul realized he viewed money as power, and when he felt powerless, he spent more money he didn't have, in hopes of avoiding that feeling. Then, terrified of exposing himself as a fraud, he frantically surrounded himself with symbols of success to keep the charade going as long as possible. He realized that this had to change completely, or he'd face jail—or worse, the kind of despair that leads to suicide.

Another member, a small woman in her sixties, Diane, admitted that for her, it felt better to put something on a credit card than it did to pay cash. Using her card, she said, made her feel like part of an elite club. She said it felt "magical." As if she'd gotten away with something. And that's precisely the effect credit card marketers are after. For Diane, paradoxically—tragically—the only way to quell the fear of having no money was to spend money she didn't really have. Eventually, she depleted her savings and cashed in her retirement funds. Then she began to beg, borrow, and steal from friends and family to keep up appearances. But soon the banks and the creditors caught up with her. In the end, she, too, was broke, homeless, and alone.

Listening to these harrowing stories, I realized that these weren't bad people. Not at all. They were clearly intelligent people who'd made very bad decisions about money and were facing the consequences. But what became apparent was the powerful allure of money and how easy it was for all these people to believe that power comes from money itself, rather than from how money is deployed.

After the meeting's close, I hung around for a while, greeting the attendees—young hipsters, middle-aged teachers, former executives—all of whom had shared their stories with me that day. I shook hands with the bike messenger who shopped compulsively on the Internet. I chatted with the actress who came to DA with $120,000 in credit card debt spent on cars and vacations, because every time she got a card, she spent to the limit, as if it were her own money. These weren't people who "didn't stick to a budget." Their spending and debt signified chronic problems that require long-term treatment and close work with a DA sponsor, someone who has broken free of the financial quagmire and is willing to help others out.

I was fascinated by the literature DA sold at a buck or two a brochure. Much of it was clear and simple advice that dovetails with the guidance I'm giving in this book. Put pen to paper. Write everything down. Have a plan. Keep meticulous records. Don't hide from your creditors. Seek help from experts. Stay financially honest. This is all excellent advice, because these habits create transparency. That leads to financial accountability and stability, which removes the mystery from money.

Fear and anxiety around money are usually the result of ignorance, of not knowing how much money you actually have, let alone where it is. Believe me, this is not a "rich people" problem. This is *not* the problem of having so much money you don't know where it is. In fact, wealthy people often know exactly what they're worth, right down to the last dollar in their wallet. They usually got rich because of meticulous money habits.

Financial ignorance is a problem that many people face, not just folks in DA. Many people are lazy when it comes to money matters, letting the banks keep their financial records; rarely, if ever, balancing their own checkbooks; or reconciling their accounts themselves. These are bad financial practices. They are what lead to the sense of powerlessness discussed in the rooms of DA. Of course, you're powerless over things about which you remain willfully ignorant.

Money Pledge

You may not need a place like Debtors Anonymous. I hope you don't. If you are like so many people out there and you are carrying some debt, follow my advice in this book and become debt-free as soon as you can. Then, move on to the next steps toward financial security: saving and investing.

I hope your money problems aren't so dire that you need a program and a sponsor. But I still want you to think of me as your Money Sponsor, someone who has been through the thick of it, who has experienced economic insecurity and has come out the other end thriving. My qualifications for being your Money Sponsor have nothing to do with having money. They have to do with my fundamental philosophies around building wealth. I have not created my wealth because I am special or different. I have never believed a lottery ticket or an inheritance will save the day.

You got through Part One, you found your 90-Day Number, you gave honest answers to some tough questions about your spending, saving, and investing, you know what it will take to live within your means, and you are ready to begin setting aside money to save and perhaps invest. Now it's time to commit, folks.

Take the money pledge below. Don't just read it, sign it. This is your promise—to yourself, to your loved ones, and to me, your Money Sponsor—that you will abide by the principles of value, discipline, and security, with an eye to improving your financial life.

Money Pledge

1. I will take a cold hard look at my current financial situation, using the ninety-day money model outlined previously in this book. I'm going to put my financial life on paper so I know exactly where I stand, because knowledge is the first step toward empowerment.

2. I will get my taxes, receipts, W-2s, bills, and insurance forms in order. I'll buy a few folders, label them, and start

organizing all my financial papers so I have easy access to them.

3. I will get everyone who is contributing financially to my household involved in this process, including my partner or spouse and any children at home receiving meaningful allowances or holding down part-time work.

4. I declare a moratorium on spending until I put down this book.

5. I will open up a no- or low-fee savings account and contribute to it every week, even if I can contribute only a small amount.

YOUR SIGNATURE HERE _____

COSIGNED BY YOUR SPONSOR _____

Part Two

YOUTH AND MONEY: LEARNING & EARNING, DATING & MATING

Rolling cash from the family Money Bowl with my son, Trevor. I used this
opportunity to talk to him about investing. I also introduced the concept of
a "Secret 10" savings account during a previous Money Bowl session.
(Savannah O'Leary)

CHAPTER 6

Kids and Cash

Sometimes I wonder if Santa Claus, the Easter Bunny, and the Tooth Fairy have done a huge disservice to our children. We've taught them that money is magic, and if they really, really want something, invisible beings will leave it for them in the night. It's crazy. And yes, I told my children the same filthy lies. But if I had to do it all over again, here is the bedtime story I'd tell them about money, while tucking them in at night.

Once upon a time, you were born and you were such a beautiful little baby. Everyone was happy when you arrived. Your parents were happy, your grandparents took pictures, but no one was happier than the Bank. That's the Bank cooing at you from behind the glass: "She's here!" said the Bank. "Our future source of unending income!"

Then you left the hospital, and the Bank didn't know where you lived. So the Bank called its friend the Government. After all, the Government issued your Social Security number, so they already had a file open on you. (They stick together, the Bank and the Government.) To the Government, you're a part of an army of citizenship, a future taxpayer. But to the Bank, you're income. When the Bank began to barrage your exhausted parents with persuasive brochures convincing them that they needed to start putting money away for their beautiful baby, it was kind of mean. But soon enough, you had a 529 college savings plan set up—all before you were even weaned.

And so it began. At first, you were a cost to your mom and dad. You needed diapers and toys, and since you didn't have a job yet, you couldn't pay for any of this stuff yourself. So they bought it for you. Then you had to get educated. More cost. So beyond the love you created in the hearts of your parents and the people around you who adored you, you didn't have any real value in the market until you became a consumer yourself.

But first, you had to go to college. So the Bank lent you a small fortune, and you were grateful for every dime. Then you got your first job. Your parents were so proud of you, and so was the Bank. They started to send you credit card notices with low introductory interest rates, and you signed up for one. Then the Bank helped you open up your first checking account so your paycheck could be automatically deposited. They weren't too interested in what you saved, hence they paid almost no interest. After that, they sold you on some mutual funds or a money market fund that also had you automatically depositing a small sum every month. All of these accounts came with fees. But you paid them, because you were trying to do the right thing with your money.

Then came your mortgage, the biggest sum of money you ever borrowed and a huge source of income to the Bank. This was the Big Kahuna, the one service the Bank had been waiting to sell you ever since you were a beautiful little baby. Most people take out a mortgage with the bank at which they first opened a savings or checking account, and that's just what you did, too. Why?

The Bank knew you, and you trusted the Bank. You'd been such a good customer so far, always making those minimum payments on your credit card, never missing a student loan payment, so the Bank gave you a pretty good rate.

But here is where the "Game of Life" begins, my dear child. At first you needed the Bank's money. You needed the student loan and the credit card and the mortgage. That's how we get ahead in life and become self-sufficient. But to win this numbers game, you have to be as ruthless as the Bank. Problem is, the Bank sets the terms of the mortgage and the level of interest you pay on your credit cards.

Getting to a place where the Bank is paying you more interest than you're paying out is the essence of growing wealth and winning the numbers game. You have to begin to tip the balance in your favor as soon as possible. But it's a relationship. Understand that there are periods where you will have to pay more interest to the Bank than it's paying you. In your twenties and thirties, when you're borrowing money for school and establishing mortgages, it's okay that the Bank's ahead. That's part of the game. But there needs to come a time when that interest starts to flow back to you, after you've paid off your mortgage and have more money to save and invest. The trick is that, over time, you want to be the one who earned more interest than you paid out. That's how you win the game. I want you to win. Some people don't get there until they're sixty or seventy years old. Some never get there. They're always servicing some kind of loan or mortgage, right to their dying day. In those cases, the Bank wins. But you can win by paying off your student loan in your twenties, remaining consumer debt–free in your thirties, and paying off your mortgage in your forties. Remember these simple rules and you'll win the game, and get you to your happily ever after:

1. Save young.
2. Scrutinize everything you buy.
3. Work while you're in school to pay down debt.
4. Invest early and often.
5. Pay down your student loan before you buy a car, or take on a mortgage.
6. Buy a home you can afford.
7. Don't grow your lifestyle along with your income.
8. Never carry credit card balances.
9. Make biweekly mortgage payments.
10. Pay down your mortgage as quickly as possible.

Doing those ten things will save you a fortune in interest payments, and get you mortgage- and debt-free faster. That's how the game of life works, and that's how you win, dear child. Knowing this, you will sleep well not just tonight, but every night. It's how you will live happily, and wealthily, ever after.

Money Mistake: You Don't Talk to Your Kids about Money

THE FIX: TEACH THEM VALUE FIRST

Babies eat and sleep, toddlers destroy everything, and kids like to spend like there's no tomorrow. And lest you think I was always a bossy bald guy, I, too, was a kid who liked things, who wanted the latest everything and would go to any length to get it.

I couldn't have been more than five years old when I first coveted something I didn't quite have enough to buy. For weeks I even visited it at the store. It was an airplane made of balsa wood, with a wind-up plastic propeller. The package said it actually flew. But it cost two dollars. For a month, I saved up money from a 50-cent-a-week allowance my mother gave my brother, Shane, and me. My grandmother was visiting us that afternoon and I proudly showed her my purchase. She took a hard look at the airplane, the way an archaeologist would scrutinize a weird relic. After a minute, she handed it back to me as if it was covered in cooties.

"Why, Kevin?" she asked.

"Why what?"

"Why did you spend two dollars on this?"

"Because I like it. I wanted it."

"But look at it, Kevin." It was as if she was pleading with me. "It's junk. It's made of nothing but scraps. It's going to fall apart after your first day playing with it."

She gave me that piercing, stern look again, making me reconsider my answer. Finally, I said, "I don't know why I bought it."

I will never forget that moment. My joy turned instantly into shame. For the first time, I actually scrutinized what I had bought—I mean, *really* looked at it. The toy (every toy) holds potent promises for kids: fun, fitting in, and friendship. That's a heady combination. That's why every commercial for a game or a toy will show kids with their friends, and the cover art of every box includes a tacit promise of fitting in with a peer group. And kids just want to fit in and be liked. Kids also want to be envied. (Having been one myself, I know a child's understanding of covetousness is almost biblical in proportion, and toy companies are masters at tapping into that primal vice.)

But my grandmother was right. Once the fancy wrapper was off and I'd put my very plain plane together, it was really just a few bits of boring wood. The toy I was going to show off and share was nothing more than a flimsy, badly constructed trinket.

It barely flew. You might think it was a little mean for Grandma to burst my bubble like that, but it became a monumental moment in my life. It was the first time I made a direct correlation between money and value.

Like any kid, I had always attached feelings to the money I spent on toys or candy. I'd see something I wanted. I'd feel sad because I didn't have it. Then I'd buy it and feel happy because I finally had what I wanted. Then the toy broke, the candy was eaten, or I got bored, only to start at the beginning again. Who doesn't cycle through that consumer thought process, child or adult? The entire advertising industry is built on putting consumers in a trance. But here was my old Lebanese grandmother breaking that spell.

I began to look at where a product was made. I considered the packaging. Kids want and buy a lot of junk. From the moment my grandmother questioned my purchase, she planted a seed in my brain, one that no longer allowed me to buy another thing in my life without asking myself these questions: Is it any good? Will it last? Where did it come from? Kids understand when something's junky. They know about crappy fast food, so teach them about cheaply made goods. If it's flimsy and built to break, tell them that. Tell them it's a waste of money, and you don't waste money. This entire lesson is undermined if you promise to buy them a cheaper version of what they want, a common parental consumer trap. If anything, you want to teach them to bargain up. Offer to pay for a portion of a better-quality item, one that will last longer and do more, if they can save up for their part. You work out the percentages based on your financial situation, but kids need to feel that transaction personally so that they can attach value to the money spent, not just to the purchased product.

Because kids eat a lot and grow fast, the majority of your money is spent on food and clothes. It usually comes out of the parent's pocket. Money for toys and games, anything you deem extra, should eventually come out of the child's pocket. What's key is to not place essentials on the same plane as extras. When your kids say, "I really need this," correct them quickly. "You *want* this, you do not need it." Teach them the difference between a need and a want. And if they attach some kind of value to the product that is disproportionate or inappropriate, say so.

Money Mistake: Your Kids Don't Understand the Value of Work

THE FIX: TEACH THEM TIME IS MONEY

I was around sixteen years old when I first discovered the relationship between time, money, and me. It snowed for twenty-six days, almost the entire month of January, which meant multiple school closings—the definition of heaven for a teen like me. My brother and I were beginning to make a pretty good income keeping our driveway clear. For the first time, my parents were paying us daily for something we used to have to do every once in a while for free. After all, we were old enough and big enough to take on this responsibility full-time. We were also earning minimum wage, which was about $1.50 an hour, and the snow was relentless. We would be drying our snow pants when another two feet would fall and we'd head back out to clear the sidewalks all over again. But it was hard, backbreaking work, even for a couple of healthy teenagers.

One day, our elderly neighbor across the street approached

us while we were clearing the last of the afternoon snow. She noticed how diligently we shoveled our own driveway and offered to pay us more to shovel hers. Shane and I looked at each other. Clearing just one driveway was hard. Doing two would be harder still, and this would leave us no time to enjoy the winter. We really didn't want to do both driveways. So the question became: Which job do we take? Do we work for our family for less than what we'd make working for our neighbor? Shane and I presented the problem to our parents. My stepfather didn't seem concerned. Surely we understood that it was more important to shovel our *own* driveway than the neighbor's.

"If you have the time and energy and want to make extra money shoveling the driveway across the street, that decision is yours to make," he said.

"That's not what we want," I blurted out. "We want a raise." We wanted what the neighbor was offering: $2.00 an hour, 50 cents more than we were getting paid by Mom and Dad. George laughed out loud and walked away. So my brother and I did what other frustrated workers around the world do: We went on strike. (Everyone's a socialist when they're young.) We stopped shoveling and went out with our friends to play in the snow.

Guess what? Our strategy worked! After a day or two, our parents negotiated our raise. Clearly, they valued not having to clean the driveway themselves, and I suspect, too, that they were trying to teach us a thing or two about money and the world of work.

We got a raise *and* worked a little overtime to help out the neighbor across the street. It was a lucrative month. (I only wish I had had the wherewithal to subcontract some of the shoveling out to friends. Now *that* would have been smart, *and* lucrative.)

Making money while shoveling snow for the neighbors in 1972.
(Georgette Kanawaty)

That January marked the first moment I understood that my time was worth money. This is a potent awareness in a young person. It's something that, as a parent, you can instill in your children from an early age. It's something that my wife, in particular, was very good at teaching our children from the moment they could walk and talk. Linda and I had no money when we got married. She had huge student loans that she paid off with her bonuses from a sales job. She worked like a dog to do that. Luckily, I married a woman for whom material things have never been that important, and she has passed that attitude on to our children. Admittedly, she was stricter with the kids regarding money, especially as they became teenagers. They weren't given an allowance. They had jobs as soon as they were old enough to work part-time—my daughter, Savannah, at a bakery when she was fourteen, and my son, Trevor, babysitting when he was eleven. (Today, at fifteen, he makes a tidy side income refurbishing not-so-old technology and selling it on the Internet.) Working part-time is how my teenagers earned money to buy the things they wanted. And the truth is, teens come to understand the true cost of goods only when they buy them themselves.

Teenagers care a lot about money, especially when they start making their own. But more than money, they care about status, brands, and being cool. A while ago, at a stoplight, I noticed a group of private-school teenagers, one of them holding a Louis Vuitton purse. I don't know if it was real or a knockoff, hers or her mother's hand-me-down, but I thought to myself how moronic it was that a teenage girl would own a $2,500 purse. That money should have been in a bank somewhere accumulating interest! (Invested once, and left to compound at 4 percent a year for fifty years, that $2,500 would be worth more than $17,000 when she turned sixty-five. Just saying.)

Listen, I was a teenager, too. When I was young, Levi's bell-bottom jeans were all the rage. I felt like Jimi Hendrix in those pants, which had a high waist, were tight at the thigh, then flared out dramatically at the calves. Every generation adopts its own must-have stuff and things that are required in order to fit in and be cool. I get it. You've probably heard it said that you know the price of everything and the value of nothing. And it was said to you as if it was an insult. But it's not an insult. It's a simple fact. Value is about consistency. It's about what things are worth over a given stretch of time. If you're a kid reading this, you haven't been around very long, so value doesn't mean much to you. It shouldn't. Time is still an abstract concept, something that only old people care about. To you, time is infinite and it moves fast. When you're a kid, it's supposed to feel that way. You grow out of clothes quickly. You get bored of games hours after you've played them a couple of times. Music goes out of style faster than you can (legally) download the next track. And with each passing year, the pace doesn't let up. Hairstyles, pant lengths and widths, and gadgets all come with expiration dates. It's the same as when I was a kid, but I will say it seems as if those dates come a lot quicker today.

Here's the problem: You haven't really owned something for five, ten, or fifteen years. You haven't watched its value increase or decrease over time. That's why teens make excellent consumers, but they suck at saving and investing—because time doesn't mean much to them.

I venture to guess that that teenaged girl wasn't worried about whether her LV bag would retain its value. I doubt it can. Why? *Because everybody will have owned that bag.* The brand will saturate the market. In ten years' time, that bag won't be worth anything.

When you're young, you think time is on your side. Time *is* on your side, but not when you're being a consumer, something teenagers are very, very good at. As a consumer, time is your enemy, and the people who make your gadgets and games know this. And they use it to their advantage. As an investor, however, when you're young, *time is your best friend.* In fact, it's the only thing you have going for you when you're young, precisely because you don't have a lot of money. Best news is, you don't need a lot of money to make great returns! You just need a future. Are you following?

Money Mistake: Saving Money Isn't as Cool as Spending It

THE FIX: YOUR "SECRET 10" IS YOUR SECRET WEAPON

Saving money is hard when you're young because young people like tangibles, labels, proof that they own something of value, something cool that everyone else wants. Saving is also hard because you don't have anything real to show for all of your discipline and sacrifice. But the hardest thing of all is saving 10 percent of your income, because to pull that off you have to pass on stuff that will gratify you immediately. So you probably don't have the newest iPad, you don't have photos from spring break, and you don't have the top-of-the-line snowboard. And when you're a teenager, that stuff matters. But so do things like power, security, and freedom. When you have money, a healthy stash that can come to your rescue at a moment's notice, you have something other kids don't. I like to call this secret stash of money the Secret 10. It's the 10 percent of your income that you're spiriting away and saving for later. It grows alongside you. Your Secret 10 accompanies you all through life, following you from your childhood bedroom to your dorm room, to the master suite, to your deathbed. It's your money, your super-power. The sooner you start setting aside that 10 percent of your income, the sooner you start to develop those powers for good use in your life. But here's another trick to preserving and grow-ing your Secret 10: Don't tell anyone about it! Not your mother, not your brother, no one. (You will have to tell your future signif-icant other, because you have to disclose this information during the prenuptial process. And you *will* listen to Uncle Kevin and get a prenup.) Because the more people who know about your Secret 10, the more vulnerable it is to be spent. By the time you get married, that Secret 10 will be significant enough that you'll want to protect it always.

Imagine a gold box with your name on it buried somewhere deep in the vaults of your trusted financial institution. Inside that box, your money is growing, changing, and waiting for you to put it to good use. Perhaps your Secret 10 will become a significant down payment on a house, or a primary source of income through a critical illness. Your Secret 10 might stay down there most of your life, coming to your rescue when you're old and gray and your kids are contemplating putting you in a nursing home. But look, you have enough money to take care of yourself in the manner that you prefer. It's your money. It's your Secret 10.

Money Mistake: You Don't Have the Discipline to Save Your Secret 10

THE FIX: MAKE SAVING AS IMPORTANT AS BRUSHING YOUR TEETH

If you are a parent of older kids, you may remember how hard it was to get your kids to brush their teeth when they were young. My mother told me I hated doing it. I used to run screaming from the bathroom. I don't remember this, but she said it was torture even getting the brush past my lips. Why did I hate brushing my teeth? I don't remember, but I was always the type of kid who didn't like being told what to do, even if it was good for me. *Especially* when it was good for me. (I'm still like that, by the way.) But here's the thing: While I don't remember those torturous tooth-brushing sessions, I do remember getting my first cavity filled. Back then, dentists' offices weren't adorned with coloring books, aquariums, and TV screens to distract terrified children. They were designed, in fact, specifically to terrify children. Dentists wore masks over their mouths and offered no reassurances that the needle wouldn't hurt. Heck, they didn't even try to hide the giant syringe! My mother was no help, sitting there with tears in her eyes as she watched the point sink into my gums. I'm not sure what hurt more—watching my mother cringe or the needle itself. Either way, this is how I learned cavities were a very, very bad thing. I never wanted another one.

After the nightmare was over, my mother and the dentist sat me down for a chat (it was a one-way conversation because my mouth was still numb). They explained that brushing my teeth more often meant I'd get fewer cavities. Fewer cavities meant fewer visits to this nightmarish place, the source of some real childhood trauma. Because of that pain and terror, I slowly began to understand that there was a connection, a tangible one, between disciplined behavior and rewards, even if the rewards really just took the form of pain avoidance. I decided to brush my teeth regularly, and eventually even learned to enjoy it.

Too bad we can't give teenagers one small financial cavity to teach them a lesson about spending and saving and the importance of building good financial habits. Teens are notoriously undisciplined (as I said before, I know because I have a couple). But teenagers are highly attuned to rewards. Consider compound-interest charts. They're numerical rewards for disciplined behavior. The dental equivalent would be a picture of a healthy smile unmarred by cavities, unthreatened by needles. As with brushing your teeth, compound-interest charts show you what's possible with disciplined behavior over time, time being the one big thing, if not the only thing, teenagers have going for them as investors.

Let's keep the numbers simple. Let's say you're not quite ready to set aside your Secret 10 yet. But you can set aside $2,000, a chunk of cash you earned over the course of the summer you turned 17 by babysitting for the family down the street. Let's look at what that $2,000 would be worth at retirement age, *if you never put in another dime.* There are two compound-interest scenarios: a conservative (and likely) average return of 3 percent over the course of 48 years, and a healthier, more optimistic return of 6 percent over 48 years, from when you're 17 to 65 years old.

YOUR STASH-AWAY CASH at Age 17	YEARLY DEPOSIT for 48 Years	VALUE @ 65 (3% Return)	VALUE @ 65 (6% Return)
$2,000	$0	$8,264.50	$32,787.74

So by this chart, it would seem that a little pain and discipline at the age of 17 will reward you with anywhere between $8,000 and $32,000 later in life, *even if you invested absolutely nothing at all, ever again.*

But what if putting aside $2,000 a year, which was hard at first and hardly noticeable later, became something you did as automatically as brushing your teeth? And you set aside $2,000 a year, every year for 48 years, because it was something you'd been doing since you were a teenager?

Let's look at *those* numbers.

AGE	PRINCIPAL	YEARLY DEPOSIT for 48 years	VALUE @ 65 3% returns	VALUE @ 65 6% returns
17	$2,000	$2,000	$223,345.80	$576,706.54

In all those years, you've progressed from being an undisciplined teenager to being someone who could be worth half a million dollars. How? By understanding that as a young person, time works to your advantage, and by insisting that saving money is as crucial to your health. You buckled down and made a few sacrifices, which were big at first—you borrowed a prom dress instead of buying a new one; you didn't backpack through Europe with your friends; you didn't own a car during college. But eventually, setting aside $2,000 a year felt as necessary as brushing your teeth. And soon it was completely painless. This saving strategy gives new meaning to a million-dollar smile.

That's compound interest, kids, the most beautiful math there is, and it was designed with you in mind. You're young. You've got beauty, strength, and vitality, but you've also got time on your side. Take advantage of it and watch your money grow.

If you are planning on having a family, make sure you partner with someone who will make up for your deficits. While I was trying to make money, my wife did a lot of work teaching our kids money smarts. *(Kevin O'Leary)*

Money Mistake: You Want Something Before You Can Afford It

THE FIX: GET CREDIT SMART BEFORE GETTING A CREDIT CARD

At seventeen, I wanted—no, *needed*—a new stereo system. And not just any stereo system. I wanted one that included a Rotel RP-1000Q turntable, a McIntosh tube amp, and Bose 801 speakers. I had a real job, working part-time hosing the crusted gunk off the sides of garbage trucks, so I could justify the purchase of a high-end stereo system, a rite of passage for most teenagers who've fallen in love with music. And it's never been enough for teens just to hear music. They have to have the perfect sound system on which to play their music, even if the system takes up a significant corner of their bedrooms and the speakers shake the very foundation of their parents' house.

The entire system I wanted back then cost $4,000. That's a lot of money now, but it was a fortune back then—the price of a brand-new domestic car. But when I imagined showing this system off to my friends, I factored that feeling into the price tag. I wasn't conscious of the high price of the brag factor back then, but I pay attention to it today, especially as a parent of two teenagers.

I didn't have $4,000 at age seventeen. I did have $1,700, about a month's pay from my glamorous garbage truck–cleaning gig. The salesman at the stereo store bent forward and scratched his head when I told him how much I had. He wanted that $1,700. So he did what every good salesperson does to part you from your money. He talked to me as though I already owned this incredible stereo system, implying that the $1,700 was a small, inconvenient, but necessary step in that process.

"That's no problem. I'll cut the price to $3,500 and you're halfway there with the down payment. You take your system home today, the rest you pay later."

These are magical words that go along with magical mathematical thinking, right? "No problem," "down payment," "pay later." I was sold. Another month of hosing off garbage trucks and this thing would be mine. And how sweet to be able to leave the store with this dream system—today! Right now!

I piled the car full of the carefully packed boxes and headed home. I cleared a corner of my bedroom and began to lovingly assemble my new stereo system. It was a beautiful moment. When everything was set up, I carefully placed the precision needle into the groove of my Emerson, Lake and Palmer album. The sound was crystalline, gorgeous, pure—as though I had bought a dozen angels and suspended them over my bed to sing right at me. My parents heard the angels and came to my bedroom door. They didn't look nearly as happy as I was. Actually, they weren't thrilled with the sound or with the price tag, once I fessed up to how much the system cost me.

"How did you afford this?" my stepfather asked.

"I have a job, remember? Don't worry about it," I said, turning up the volume.

Nothing could dampen my enthusiasm. I felt I had purchased a source of joy, that I had made my first discerning, adult purchase, one that reflected my style, taste, and musical knowledge, which would net me the admiration of my friends and perhaps attention from girls for several counties around. My stepfather sighed, and he and my mother turned away, closing my bedroom door behind them.

The next week, I got laid off.

It's funny how something you love can become a source of

simmering resentment within moments. I loved my stereo system that morning. A few days later, I entered my room at night, and instead of seeing a source of joy, I began to see a shiny stack of anxiety. Now what? The store wanted the rest of the money in a month, which had now shrunk to three weeks. If I didn't pay on time, I would begin to be charged 16 percent interest, compounded monthly. My $3,500 bargain would become $4,000, even $5,000, in no time.

After experiencing a few days of awful panic, I did what a lot of teenagers do. I approached my parents to ask them to bail me out. I hadn't told them about the payment plan, only what I'd spent. The idea that I had something in my possession that wasn't fully paid for was anathema to my folks, especially my mother.

I explained my choices with great humility. Then I told them I had lost my job and that I needed to pay off the balance on the stereo or face crippling interest charges.

"Kevin, have you lost all good sense?" my mother said. "I can't believe that any son of mine would do something so foolish with his money. George, can you believe this?!" My parents looked at each other.

"Please," I said. "I need you to pay for the rest of the stereo."

Then, without exchanging so much as a word, my parents gave me a firm answer: "No."

Poor Shane. My brother was younger than me and always good with money. I went to him next. (See why I say borrowing money from family is fraught with problems? But hey, I was young then, and didn't know any better.) I pleaded, I begged, I told him he was the best brother in the world. In the end, he helped me out. Then, I got another job and I paid him back over the course of several months, with no interest. But I will never forget the emotional turmoil that that purchase created in me: from the heady opiate of owning something with so much power and promise, to the gut-wrenching fear that same purchase produced when I realized I couldn't afford what I had wanted so badly. What a terrible disconnection: to have something in my possession that wasn't really mine, and yet to be unable to give it back. And yet, this is a state that a lot of people exist in, day in and day out, people with massive credit card debt, who screen their calls, who consistently live beyond their means. I was lucky that my decision wasn't catastrophic. But I was shaken. I had put myself in jeopardy. I felt it to my core. And yet I also know that at the time, I was powerless to resist that stereo.

Since then, I have never carried a credit card balance. I have never paid only the minimum payment, because in my mind I began to double the price of everything I bought with a credit card. If a pair of skis cost $500, in my head I made them cost $1,000. "Now can you afford them?" I asked myself. From that moment on, credit was about convenience only. It was never a shortcut to consumer joy.

So I know how easy it is to get caught up in that whirlwind of consumer enthusiasm. When you stand in front of something you want, you can feel the beginnings of consumer intoxication taking effect. It's powerful when it's mixed with teenage hormones, which is precisely how big-box electronic stores can get young people to make big purchases. Those places are like nightclubs, with pounding music and visual overload at every turn. Gadgets are how teens measure their coolness and value. It was true when I was kid and it's true now. Everything's all about bigger, better, and faster. It always was. And it's impossible not to get caught up in spending way more than you can afford, because "want" takes over for "need." And here's the crazy part: We let it happen.

But here's the true litmus test to determine whether you're ready to get a credit card and start building your credit rating: When you understand the difference between buying something necessary and buying stuff you don't need but really want, you know you're ready to begin using a credit card.

Money Mistake: You Think Credit Cards and Financial Services Are Free

THE FIX: BE AWARE OF HIDDEN FEES AND INTEREST

A plastic card, or layaway plans, can stimulate a lot of magical thinking in a teenager, and generate a lot of ignorance. For the young folks reading this, I suggest you do not get or use a credit card until you understand a basic savings account and debit card and know how to use a checking account. You can even practice by first getting comfortable using a prepaid card for at least a year so you fully understand a spending and billing cycle. But be aware of the phenomenal amount of fees attached to those cards. Prepaid cards are being used more and more in lieu of checking accounts by people who are fleeing high fees from banks. But you still have to pay to put money on those prepaid cards. So always read the fine print. Speaking of which, check out your credit card bill, where it tells you how long it will take you to pay off a balance if you're making only minimum payments. Banks and credit card companies are required to post that information, because in some cases a seemingly manageable amount—like, say, $2,000—can still take several years to pay off, if you're making only the minimum payment.

The most important thing you need to understand is that when you get a credit card, you're allowing the banks and credit card companies an inside look at your spending habits. You're effectively saying to a bank, "You're now allowed to make judgments and decisions about my financial worth based on what I do with this card." The bank or credit card company is now your official financial monitor. So you have to start monitoring *them*. Watch for hidden fees, scrutinize your bill, and know that everything any financial institution does for you costs something, somewhere.

But the best way to understand the punitive nature of interest rates and fees is to see them at work. I accidentally stumbled onto a concrete way to demonstrate how painful it is to lose a big portion of my money in fees when I took my son, Trevor, to try out one of those green coin counters at the local grocery store a couple of years ago. We have something we call the Money Bowl. Over the years, whenever we have loose change in our pockets, we put it in the Money Bowl. So a while ago, I noticed that the massive bowl was getting quite full. I was pretty sure we had about $500 just sitting there, and I thought this would be a great project to get Trevor involved in. Counting out all that change by hand would have taken ages, so Trevor and I headed to the local grocery store with the Money Bowl. I had heard that these machines quickly counted the coins and issued a receipt that you took to the checker in exchange for the cash in bills. All you had to do was drop the coins in a tray and let the machine do the rest. So that's what we did. Fistful by fistful, we dropped coins into a tray while the machine tallied everything up. After about twenty minutes of doing this, the Money Bowl was empty. Great! Job completed. But it wasn't until the machine spat out a receipt that I realized it had charged us a whopping 9.8 percent "counting fee." I couldn't believe my eyes. To say I was furious is an understatement.

"Dad, what's wrong?" Trevor asked, picking up on the expression of shock that was writ large across my face.

"I can't believe this," I said. And then I explained to my son that we'd been had.

"But that's totally unfair!" was his response. "We have to fight this."

So, knowing that I hadn't read the fine print on the machine before inserting our coins, I decided to fight the fees. I complained to the manager, my son standing next to me.

"I just paid a big green machine almost $50 to count coins for me," I said. "My son would have done it for $10."

"Yup," the manager said. "Buyer beware."

"So you can't lower the fee at all?" I asked. "That's robbery!"

"Like I said, buyer beware."

The company that owned the machine set the fees, not the store. I should have known that. I looked at Trevor, who seemed totally dumbfounded. I was upset about the loss of $50 to a stupid machine, but I was glad of one thing: My son had learned an important lesson about reading the fine print, and so had I!

Call me cheap, but I thought about that lost money for two days. Since that fiasco, Trevor and I have accumulated another big bowl of money, and guess what we did with it the second time? We went to Staples, bought an inexpensive coin-rolling kit, and did everything ourselves. Luckily, I love money, so I find the whole exercise relaxing.

Test Your Child's Money Smarts

I have a wealthy friend who's conducting an interesting experiment. He has decided to give each of his kids their inheritance, a quarter of a million dollars, when they turn eighteen. But that's it. That's the only money they'll ever receive from him. It's his way of transferring wealth early to kids who are going to receive the money eventually. But he's doing it now, because he believes that if his children are bad with money, if they squander it, it's better to know that sooner rather than later. And it's how he hopes they'll learn how to manage, invest, and budget effectively.

My jury's out on his method, but I do agree that you should make it a point to watch how your children and teens handle money. Here's a Q&A that will help you get a handle on your child's financial habits so you can help correct the bad ones.

1. **If you send your child to buy something with your money, does he or she automatically give you the change, or do you have to ask for it?**

   This is a revealing transaction. When my wife gives my son cab fare to return from a party, her hand is out the minute he arrives home. If there's change, it goes back in her wallet. She considers that cab trip on her, if she can't pick him up herself. That money, however, is not his, and it's not meant to be used any other way. Good money boundaries, understanding who pays for what, are crucial. You don't want your children to grow up to be the kind of jerks who don't put in their fair share for a big restaurant bill. I suspect those people grew up with bad money boundaries. Regardless of their excuse, I don't eat a second meal with anyone who cheaps out. Learning how to make change is also as crucial as memorizing multiplication tables. As soon as your kid knows what money is, sit him or her down and do some basic money math.

2. **If, after hearing you say you couldn't afford something he or she wanted, has your child ever suggested you put it on a credit card? Or asked you to pay for it, with the promise of paying you back from his or her savings when you get home?**

    If your kid is too old to wash his or her mouth out with soap, this is an opportunity for a serious sit-down. It's important to tell your kids that credit cards are good for only two things: to save you from having to carry cash, and to establish a credit rating. That's it. They must lose the idea, right from the get-go, that credit cards are magic, a different kind of money. As for on-the-spot purchases, this is a good opportunity to teach your kids about delayed gratification. If they're not prepared to purchase something, because they've left their money at home, then it'll have to wait until another trip to the mall.

3. **Does your child gaze through catalogues, websites, or magazines pointing out all the things he or she wishes to have?**

    Kids love things and stuff, and when they're young, there's something fantastical about pointing at a picture and the toy suddenly appearing under a tree or on their birthday. But this is an opportunity to begin showing kids the difference between a need and a want. Needs are things like food and clothing. Wants are toys and games. And then there are the big-screen TVs they wish they had on the wall in their rooms, and the $3,000 tricked-out Mac that, if they want, they'll have to buy themselves someday. Parents must make their own decisions about what to spend on holiday and birthday presents. But your family budget shouldn't be a thing of mystery. When planning finances and setting aside money for special occasions and shared purchases, include the kids as soon as possible. When they start to understand what money is, they should also begin to learn about spending and saving as well. Don't offer to pay the difference for things they can't quite afford yet, or you'll undo all the lessons you're trying to teach.

4. **Does your child offer to do chores and jobs around the house in exchange for money or extra allowance (if you're already tying chores to money)?**

I don't like equating money with doing work around the house that should be done by members of the family at no cost. When we gave our kids money, it wasn't tied to taking out the garbage or picking up after themselves. If there was work to do around the house, it was done. An allowance was separate. What happens when you tie chores to money is you also make it possible for kids to get lazy and forgo cash in order to skip vital tasks. *"I don't feel like walking the dog today, so take it off my allowance."* As a parent, that leaves you without a powerful bargaining chip. If you want to give your children an allowance, make it consistent. When they're around seven years old and learning to reason, begin to show them how (and why) to set aside a certain amount in savings. Show them how to budget their money so it lasts. And help them make smarter purchases.

5. **Has your child ever compared your house, car, or belongings to those of your wealthier neighbor or friend?**

Even though I grew up all over the world in very different socioeconomic environments, I was never made aware that we had more than the children we played with in Cambodia, Cyprus, Ethiopia, Switzerland, or Tunisia. George and my mother encouraged us to hang with the local children, and not just other so-called diplomatic brats. That had a way of blurring money lines between us. It wasn't until we were back from living abroad that I began to notice when the neighbors bought a brand-new car or had gone to Disneyland over Christmas. But when I'd tell my parents by way of wanting to prod something similar out of them, they'd just shrug and say, "That's nice for them." They weren't the "keeping up with the Joneses" type of parents.

So next time your child runs into the house declaring that the next-door neighbor just got the latest Xbox, use it as an opportunity to explain how unimportant all that stuff is, and that competing for neighborhood prominence using pools, cars, and video consoles isn't a game you play.

Kids pick up on their parents' attitudes about money. If you and your partner have a healthy relationship with money, and can speak openly and freely about what money is and isn't, then chances are good your child will absorb those positive messages. But if money is a central complaint in the family, and your fights revolve around the lack of money, or bad spending habits, then you might be sending dangerous messages about money.

CHAPTER 7

The High Cost of Higher Education

Postsecondary education is important; it gives you an edge. So it's hard to argue against more schooling, and it's something I won't do. Education has its own intrinsic value, and sometimes that doesn't necessarily translate into money. Many graduates end up with degrees that don't necessarily lead to lucrative careers, let alone the easy ability to pay back their student loans. That's why I believe education is education right up until you enter a postsecondary institution. After that, education becomes an investment, one that should be as carefully considered as where you're going to buy your first house. (Or *if* you're going to buy one. This is not a given.)

It varies from state to state, but tuition for an in-state undergraduate degree program costs, on average, between $4,000 and $15,000 a year. If you go to college out of state, the national average skyrockets to nearly $22,000. And if you've got your heart set on a private college or university, get ready to pay *at least* $29,000. The cost of grad school is even more formidable—you're looking at close to $30,000 if you study medicine or law, $37,000 if you want to be a dentist. These numbers don't include books, fees, room and board, transportation, or recreation, all of which add tens of thousands to the final bill. So after doubling and tripling some of those numbers, it wouldn't be uncommon for an average twenty-three-year-old with, say, a master's degree in education to graduate more than $100,000 in debt.

That's a horribly depressing way to start out your young life. But here's the common rationalization of that kind of debt: *I'll get a good job and in no time I'll pay that off.* The problem is, young people in this country are discovering that the job market isn't always greeting them with open arms after they pick up their degrees. And if they do get jobs, they're often not in their field of study, or are entry-level positions that don't pay all that much. So many young graduates are trapped in that awful place where their debt is growing faster than their ability to pay it off. Their student loan becomes this ugly thing that follows them around after college and right into their first marriages. The loan gets in the way of buying a car or a house. It's just always *there.* Lucky you if Mom and Dad socked away enough money for your postsecondary education and you were perfectly happy to live at home for those four years, saving a ton of money. That's not the reality for most students. More than half of students in postsecondary school will graduate with debt.

Nursing, law, dentistry degrees—all these are good investments, because these degrees generally mean a well-paying job is in the offing upon graduation, one that'll help you tackle the hideous debt you'll accumulate before graduation. But again, like any investment, even those so-called sure things are risky.

What about a general liberal arts degree? It's nice to have, but it's not a great investment, because there's often no clear-cut job waiting for you at the end, since you haven't learned a real, tangible skill, like surgery or accounting. I say this as someone with an undergraduate degree in psychology and environmental studies. College was fun. I learned a lot. But I was completely unprepared for the job market when I graduated. Lucky for me, my parents were paying for my education, so I didn't graduate $60,000 in debt after studying trees and bones for four years. Luckier still, my stepfather sat me down and convinced me that an MBA would save my bacon after blowing four years pursuing my interests.

This will be an unpopular statement, but I am directly addressing it to young people who are paying out of pocket for their education: Imagine the end result of your degree and plan backward. Fine arts might be your passion, but consider the kind of work you want to do when you graduate, because the cold hard truth is that for much of your adult life, you're going to be working, so it better be doing something you like, and it better be something that's going to make you enough money for you to be happy. Better yet, it should be enough money that you'll have extra to spend on your interests. This isn't about ignoring your passions. Photography has been my passion since I was a teenager. But when I announced to my parents that my plan was to be a photographer, my stepfather sat me down for a little talk.

He said, "It's good that you know what you want to *be*, but what do you want to *do* for a living?"

I didn't understand. Do? Be? I didn't realize there was a difference.

"Do you have any idea what you have to *do* in order to be a photographer?" he asked. I scratched my head.

"Let's put it this way," he continued. "How much money do you think you'll need to make to be happy?"

I pulled a figure out of my head: $20,000, which was a decent income back then. George laughed. He explained that most photographers, starting out, don't make that kind of money. Then he explained the harsh realities of following my passion as a career instead of as an outlet.

"You might not be good enough, Kevin, and the wrong time to find that out is on the other side of a big debt."

If I sound like I'm discouraging genuine talent, I'm not. In fact, I don't think it's really possible to do that. I am discouraging people from committing to expensive degrees from colleges and universities that sell a pipe dream. *"Study this and you'll be guaranteed a job!"* Remember this, kids: Colleges and universities are businesses. Even though many are structured like charities and have loftier mandates than corporations, colleges have bottom lines and ever-increasing operating costs. They have to fill desks, too.

So before you commit to an expensive course of action, take a lesson from my stepfather. He taught me that if I knew how to *do* something, I could *be* anything. Want to be a photographer? Great, go to business school and get your MBA as a fallback. Want to be a writer? Get your journalism degree, and make sure to take the technical courses as well, such as editing and camera operating, just to be safe. Want to act? Get a teaching degree and you'll have a rapt audience all day long, and you can audition at night or during your long summer holidays.

Your education can be the best investment you'll ever make, or the worst one. It's an expensive and time-consuming undertaking. And make no mistake—it is an investment. It's not a break between childhood and adulthood, or an opportunity to take it easy before real life kicks in. Every dollar you spend on postsecondary education has to be viewed in terms of its financial return. Getting smart costs money, so don't be a dummy.

Money Mistake: You Bought Fancy Wheels to Match Your Fancy Education

THE FIX: TWO WHEELS GOOD, FOUR BAD

You don't need a car when you're a student. Plain and simple. You need time to study. So you had a car in high school? Great—sell it and give your Secret 10 a nice boost. "But Uncle Kevin," you say. "I have to commute to college." Fine. That's what public transit is for: for reading textbooks! A young person who owns a car and has a student loan is setting him- or herself up for financial ruin. Between insurance, gas, parking, and repairs, you are bleeding money. If commuting is a problem, live closer to campus. Get a bunch of roommates and rent a house. Find a part-time job near the school. Saving money should be as important as your grades right now. Don't like my advice? Then you won't like this either: Get a bike. It's cheaper than public transit.

Strictly from a financial point of view, cars are ridiculous money pits (more on that in Chapter 13). Pollution and global warming aside, as gas prices go up and up, a car is becoming more and more of a luxury product rather than a given. But North America has a love affair with the car. According to the most recent numbers out of the U.S. Bureau of Labor Statistics and Consumer Spending, people spend more money keeping their cars on the road than they do putting food on the table. Even the venerable *Wall Street Journal*, in the middle of the 2008 recession, advocated that cash-strapped families consider dumping their cars to save money.

If you have to commute to campus, buy an electric bike instead of a car. I love them. They're rapidly growing in popularity in car-congested cities in China, and I expect they'll be a massive trend in North America as well. Unlike Vespas or scooters, which are mingled in with the rest of the traffic, you can stay in a safer bike lane and still park for free with a good lock. You can travel more than sixty miles with one overnight charge of a high-powered lithium battery at a cost of about 25 cents. And if it runs out of power, most e-bikes switch back to a regular bike automatically. They're pricey—anywhere from $1,500 to $4,000—but that's probably your used-car budget. Unlike a car, the bike will hold its value and pay for itself in a year. You'll stay fit and save a fortune.

Driving my mother's car near our home in Switzerland in 1970. She taught me that you don't want to own one until you are employed. *(Georgette Kanawaty)*

Money Mistake: You Don't Have Time to Work and Study

THE FIX: GET THE RIGHT PART-TIME JOB

I'm going to sound like an old guy here, but when I was in school, kids worked. They didn't spend four to six hours a night on Facebook or playing video games. They worked in bars and restaurants near the campus and they lived with a pile of room-mates, some sleeping on a cot in the hallway. That's just how it was. That's how you saved a buck. I monetized my shuffleboard hobby and made a killing playing three nights a week against other players in local pubs. Even if you have to lighten your study load and graduate in five rather than four years, it's better to do that than accumulate a massive debt.

Time is money as a student. Restaurant work also means tips, cash, and, nine times out of ten, it pays more than standing around in a store shilling jeans and shoes. Malls wind down at nine or ten o'clock at night, and so does a dinner shift in an average restaurant. But unlike the mall job, your restaurant job puts more cash in your pocket working the same number of hours. Some parents might have a problem with my encouraging kids to work in bars or restaurants. Get over it. If he or she is slinging beer for money, it means your precious child is not blowing money on beer and doesn't have enough time to drink it. But whether it's The Gap or Outback Steakhouse, kids: Get a job; just get one. Trust me, you have the time; you're just not allocating it properly.

I'll go even further. Even *after* you graduate and get a foot-hold in the nine-to-five work world, keep your part-time job at that restaurant or bar a couple of nights a week. Use that extra money to pay down your debt. Deal with balance and quality-of-life issues after you get out of debt. But while you're in debt, you're a hamster on a wheel. That also means having roommates to keep your rent low, watching movies at home (it's cheaper), and eating takeout instead of at fancy restaurants (or better yet, learning to cook—probably good for your love life, too). One of the big secrets to growing wealth is never changing your fundamental lifestyle as the money piles up. Don't change your lifestyle until your income levels rise. If you listen to all of this advice now, believe me, your thirties will thank you.

My college roommates and me in 1974. We packed five people into this two-bedroom dump to minimize costs and try to stay out of debt! *(Property of Kevin O'Leary)*

Money Mistake: You Think Postsecondary Education Is the Only Option

THE FIX: THINK OUTSIDE THE CUBICLE

It's drilled into our heads when we're young: You have to go to college to get a good job. Without a college education, you're going to live at home for the rest of your life. It's not true! Don't fall into the trap of thinking you have to be a tycoon, banker, lawyer, dentist, or doctor to have money. You might need a college degree for those jobs. And if a career like that is your dream, pursue it, by all means. But not everyone *should* go to college. In fact, colleges and universities tend to create excellent employees, but if you want to make a great living, be your own boss, provide for your family, and have enough to retire well—and if you're at all entrepreneurial—consider the trades.

Plumbers, electricians, repair specialists, mechanics, chefs—these are jobs that are always in demand, are fairly mobile, and, most important, pay well. So think outside the cubicle. Think beyond the "office box." Skilled trades don't require years and years of expensive schooling, and if you do graduate with debt, it'll likely be manageable. My favorite part of choosing a trade: Many of the best tradespeople go into business for themselves, in turn employing the young graduates as apprentices in their companies.

I like entrepreneurs, and I like trades as a vocation a lot, because you're still pursuing a higher education, which I insist on, but this path casts an eye toward the bigger picture. So if you're wishy-washy about your future and going to college only because your friends are, it could be the single biggest mistake you make, especially if you're footing the bill through a six-figure loan. And if you're resisting the vocational path because of some misguided stigma against trades, get over it. I've never met a poor, unhappy plumber who works for him- or herself. Let's face it: If you're realistic, you might not even be college material. I certainly wasn't. I have an irrepressible entrepreneurial streak that, luckily, was nurtured by my parents and my mentors. I got through college, sure, but I now know it wasn't the only option.

According to the U.S. Bureau of Labor Statistics, employees made an average hourly wage of $23.73. Compare that to $24.92, the national average for plumbers, or $25.44, the average hourly wage for an electrician. These tradespeople earn an average hourly wage 5 to 7 percent higher than other professions. Many of them also work for themselves, set their own hours, and hire and fire their teams. And they make a lot more money when they work for themselves or work in certain areas. Case in point: There are only a few big contracting companies in the lake-house community where I own a summer home. In many instances, the contractors' homes are much bigger than those owned by their supposedly richer clients. After getting a bill for the renovations on my boathouse, I can see why that's the case.

There's also this dichotomy to consider: According to a 2012 report from the Brookings Institution, 76 percent of available jobs require some form of postsecondary education. But the percentage of jobs that require a *degree* is only 43 percent. (And don't forget that 100 percent of those student loans have to be paid back.) So the chances of finding gainful employment with a diploma instead of a degree are tipped in your favor. Then there's the fact that tradespeople are in increasing demand; the McKinsey Global Institute predicts that employers around the world will need nearly 45 million more medium-skill laborers (workers with secondary school and vocational training) by 2020. This potential disaster is an incredible opportunity for entrepreneurial tradespeople.

In the end, the best thing about the trades is that they're creative. You're working with your hands, you're making and doing something tangible, and you're sometimes working outdoors. If this lifestyle suits you, go for it.

Quiz: Are You Ready for the High Cost of Higher Ed?

Kids, this one's for you. If you're considering postsecondary education, take this quiz first and see if it really is the best next step for your future.

1. **In high school, you were the kind of student who:**
   a) slept in, skipped classes, and was more interested in your weekend plan than your teacher's lesson plan. You know you're not stupid, even though some of your teachers thought you were. It's just that to be engaged, you need to be doing something hands-on.
   b) did the bare minimum, just enough to get by unnoticed and unchallenged, but loved working part-time jobs in the "real" world, where you learned practical skills and where people you worked with praised your work ethic.
   c) loved school and classes and joined every extracurricular activity, knowing it would benefit you in the future.
   d) made the honor roll without fail, and put your grades before anything else, including any fun.

If you answered D, you're probably well suited for college; high school was just a temporary stop on your way to higher education. Choose the school and your course load wisely, and remember: The fact that you were a superstar in high school doesn't mean you'll shine in college. Be competitive and don't lose that edge. Choose your major with care, because dropping classes and changing course loads adds up.

If you answered C, you certainly have the discipline for college, but if your dream job doesn't require a postsecondary degree, then consider skipping it in favor of a trade or opening a business. You like to work and you have a social streak. You already know you're good at talking to people and probably good at team-building, too. The ranks of successful entrepreneurs who never went to postsecondary school are legion. Think clearly about the postsecondary decision before you take on massive debt.

If you answered A or B, then I must say, I was just like you. Still, I went to college. It was the right choice in the end for me, but it might not be for you. Discipline can be learned, and you'll need it if you want to get the best bang for your tuition buck. But if you've taken my advice to heart, I hope you'll see that not choosing to pursue a college degree isn't in any way a failure. Your path to financial well-being is as golden as any undergrad's, maybe even more so, provided you develop your own skills in a suitable direction. Again, I ask you, have you considered the trades?

2. **You chose your college or university based on:**
   a) the awards, scholarships, and financial aid package they offered you.
   b) proximity. It was the closest one to home and you aren't going to be living on campus.

c) where your friends were accepted. It's your first time away from home, after all, and you wouldn't want to give up your social life.

d) the brochure. Everyone in the glossy photos looked like they were having a good time.

e) the fact that it was the only school that accepted you.

If you picked A and you answered C or D to question 1, good for you. You're a good fit for college and you're making good use of all the perks and gifts the institution of your choice offers.

If you chose B, maybe your priority is to graduate without debt. But make sure you do a cost/benefit analysis if you're also going to need a car to commute back and forth to campus. Between parking, insurance, upkeep, and gas, you may not be saving all that much money by skipping the dorm option or a shared house nearby.

If you chose C, D, or E, imagine buying a house based on a picture, or moving to a city you've never been to just because a couple of your friends live there. You'd never do that. Understand the enormous commitment before you take it on, or delay enrollment until you're sure you can handle the academic responsibility and the financial burden.

3. **In order to afford college, you've financially prepared yourself by:**
   a) thanking your parents for setting aside a lot of their own hard-earned money in the form of a healthy college fund that you can now tap into.
   b) getting your grades high enough to qualify for every scholarship and award there is, eliminating some of the financial burden on your parents.

     c) diligently filling out loan applications from banks
       willing to finance your entire education.

     d) working part-time all year round at that mall, or
       weekends at that restaurant, just to pay your own way.

If you answered A, you're a lucky dog. You have parents who are able, or at least willing, to foot the bill for your postsecondary education. And if they're willing to support you during school so you don't have to have a job that will distract you from your studies, all the more fortunate. Get good grades, graduate at the top of your class, and at least demonstrate it was a great investment for them.

If you answered B, good for you. You used your smarts to reap financial rewards. Keep finding ways to do that, and you're set for life.

If you answered C, then at least be certain this is the kind of investment you want to make in yourself. A loan is a huge responsibility, your first one, so don't take it on lightly.

If you answered D, then I admire your fortitude. Still, there's nothing wrong with taking six months or a year *after* high school to work and save some more money. No one says you have to graduate when you're twenty-one or twenty-two. If working for a year means not carrying a heavy debt load, or not working too hard while studying, then by all means I suggest you delay college, especially if it means curbing your debt load later.

4. **You've decided that your living arrangements at college will be:**
     a) very manageable—financially, at least—because you've
       picked a school close to home and will therefore stay in
       your old room.

b) dorm-room style. And you're hoping the school matches you up with a decent roommate.

c) a shared apartment. You've met three strangers on Craigslist and you're sharing the cost of a house.

d) the last thing you're going to scrimp on. You deserve luxury, and you need it in order to pull off good grades. That's why you're splurging on that awesome off-campus pad.

No matter what option you circled, housing is going to be your biggest cost, so keep your needs minimal and your overhead low.

If you answered A, remember that living at home does not mean a free ticket. To be a responsible adult means contributing to your household in ways that you didn't when you lived there in high school. And you can't bring the party home with you. On the bright side, you're going to be less distracted.

If you answered B, remember that dorm rooms mean minimal kitchen facilities and a lot of takeout, which could amp up the overhead, not to mention the poundage. Keep one eye on the wallet and the other on the scale.

If you answered C, get a breakdown of finances in writing. Roommate situations are fraught with money issues. In fact, it's about the only thing I remember fighting over during my college years: who pays for what and who owes money to whom.

If you answered D, I'm sorry, but you need to listen very carefully to Uncle Kevin. I'm concerned. Yes, the idea of splurging on an awesome apartment during college is tempting, but consider how little time you'll actually spend there. In fact, if you're taking out a hefty loan, this is the wrong place to spend the majority of your cash. Learning to live with roommates and to compromise are key skills that will come in handy in later years. Save your money and bunk up. It's only for a few years.

5. **To keep spending under control during your college years, your plan is to:**
   a) live like a pauper, make friends with ramen noodles, wash your clothes in the sink, and eat as many meals as possible at home.
   b) budget like crazy, never buying on credit, keeping an eye on every cost, saying no to every extra, and buying used books only.
   c) relegate student loans and any money set aside for school-related items only, using income from part-time jobs to pay for any extras, and pooling resources with other friends for meals and entertaining.
   d) hang around the wealthiest people you can find so they'll pick up the tab. And splurge on ski trips and bar nights. You're not just getting educated, you're creating memories to last a lifetime, right? Aren't they also part of the postsecondary experience?

Every campus is booby-trapped to snag your money: dorm-room upgrades, campus bars, takeout places, convenient bookstores, and the need to look your best among your peers.

If you answered A, try to live a little. Deprivation can also breed resentment, so enjoy the odd meal out and treat yourself when you hit those academic benchmarks.

If you answered B or C, you're keeping your eye on your cash flow, and that's good. Say no to big-ticket items like a car or a big-screen TV, and keep your spending proportionate to your input. We all know the stories of student loans financing spring break vacations and new iPads. That's how you graduate with crippling debt as opposed to manageable debt.

If you answered D, listen carefully: College is not an excuse to abuse people's generosity. Nor is it an excuse to foolishly spend your loan or your parents' income. College is the worst time to create more of that dreaded Ghost Money.

———

Postsecondary education is one of the most important investments you'll ever make. Going to college because you have nothing better to do, or just because your friends are going, is a foolish waste of money. Get serious about it or delay until you know exactly what you want to study, where you should go, how you'll earn money when you're there, and how to increase your chances of getting a job when you graduate. This isn't about continuing the party that started in high school. It's about laying the groundwork for your financial future.

CHAPTER 8

Boomers and Boomerangs: When Generations Financially Collide

The Boomerang Generation is a difficult subject to broach with many parents who've welcomed their adult children home after years of postsecondary education. It's not always a joyous homecoming. Usually, the reason behind the move is that their child can't find a good job, let alone one that'll pay enough to cover bills and mounting student loan payments. A recent U.S. Census Bureau report claimed the percentage of young men who moved back home went from 14 percent in 2005 to 19 percent in 2011. It's no coincidence that the economy took a significant nosedive starting around 2008.

To the young adults out there moving back home: I understand why it's all too tempting to reclaim the ease and comfort of your old bed and the video-game console in your parents' basement. But here's the problem: It's crippling your parents financially. The Children's Mutual, a U.K. company that manages savings and investments for children, did a survey in 2010. It found that many parents who support their children between the ages of eighteen and thirty do so at considerable cost to their own financial health. As many as a third reportedly remortgaged their homes to help their adult children. Two-thirds said they made other adjustments, such as selling a car and cutting back on groceries and utility costs to financially assist their kids. Worse, fully 16 percent of those parents *expected* to spend this kind of money. This is insane.

Why are parents decimating their savings to help their kids? I have a theory: They're probably part of the baby boom generation. They have good jobs, mortgages almost fully paid up, and money in the bank. They feel guilty about their good fortune while their own children suffer. But when parents jeopardize their own financial health in the name of helping their children, they're just courting financial disaster down the road. They're putting their own retirement in jeopardy. It'll come back to haunt them later.

I direct these next few paragraphs toward adult children who've moved home and are taking advantage of their parents' goodwill, living at home for free, cashing their checks, eating their food. Your parents don't seem to have the guts to tell you this, but *they don't really want you to move back home. Not because they don't love you. They do. But because they can't afford it.* Their focus should be on their financial health and socking away enough for their retirement. Not on keeping you comfortable and happy. That's *your* job.

And here's another truth, kids: Bunking in with your folks when the going gets tough deprives you of the chance to realize your potential and learn the important grown-up lesson of how to get through bad times. That's how true self-esteem is established: by doing estimable acts *for others*, not by hearing how amazing and wonderful you are from people who are going to say those things no matter what. By "failing to launch," as it's called, you never understand what it costs to be alive in your times. Therefore, you don't develop critical muscles you need to thrive in a bad economy. Sorry, I know a lot of things suck, and the economy is one of them right now, but you've got to work with it somehow.

If you haven't made the big leap backward yet, there are a few preventive measures you can take now. And don't kid yourself: Moving back home is a step in the wrong direction. Normally, I don't suggest that you borrow any money from family, ever, but your folks may rather lend you enough money to ride out a tough time than have you move back home. Offer to pay it back at a reasonable rate, with some interest. Moving is pricey. Use the loan to pay rent and bills, and meanwhile, work like a dog. Work like two dogs, in fact. Get a second job. But by all means, stop spending so much money.

Often, the chief reason young people get into dire financial straits right out of college is that they live as if they're making the kind of money they'll make in a decade. I tell you, it's a little unsettling when I go out with my wife to an expensive restaurant and I see tables full of eighteen- to twenty-year-olds blowing $40 each on an entrée. Good for them if they can afford it. But it's the wrong thing to be spending their money on, regardless. They should be at home (their *own* home, not their parents'), barbecuing with friends and socking that extra money away.

Historically, in tough economic times, a massive population shift was a critical way of fixing things. When there are no jobs in Michigan or Nevada, the country sends a message: Move to a city where jobs *are* aplenty. "Go West, Young Man" was a phrase coined in the late 1800s. It appeared on posters up and down the Eastern Seaboard, when cities were teeming with unemployed, restless young men recently returned from the Civil War. Instead of moving back home, find your "West" and go there.

Money Mistake: You Moved Back Home with Your Parents

THE FIX: BE PROACTIVE, PRODUCTIVE, AND, ABOVE ALL, GRATEFUL

Let's say it's too late—you've moved home. This is, after all, a purely financial decision. Very few twenty-two-year-old women or men relish the thought of watching TV with their parents and asking for permission to "sleep at a friend's house." It's demoralizing. So if this is you, I'm going to assume you did everything in your power to avoid this fate. Now it's time to get out of this situation as soon as possible. Let's be clear: We're talking about a temporary return to find your footing, or to recover from sudden job loss or illness. After all, that's what family does for one another. So don't feel guilty, but give yourself a deadline. Have it in writing *before* you approach Mom or Dad with your request to move back home. I can't stress this enough. Not having a plan means burning a lot of idle years in your pajamas. Food appears magically on a plate in front of you, laundry's folded and on your bed, and your parents are a lot nicer than they used to be. Snap out of it. This is not your home. This is a way station, a temporary resting spot until you find your footing.

Make sure you're paying for something—anything. Even if your parents offer, even if they insist that you can move back home for free, remember, nothing's free, not even this. Look at it this way: For every dime your parents spend to support you past eighteen, that's a dime they won't have when they're over sixty-five. Who's going to have to chip in then? You. So put some money in an account for them, whatever you can afford. Give it to them when you leave for good, or surprise them later when it's accumulated some interest.

Then, don't just sit there. Take out the garbage and mow the lawn. Do those dishes, cook that dinner, and drive your folks or siblings around to their appointments. When you move back home, the only advantage for your parents is that they have a young, healthy helper around as they head into their later years.

And be sure to bring all your technical savvy with you. Be useful. Update computer programs, clean out old files, show your folks how to use the latest technology, or tutor younger siblings.

Then get out there and find out what your old friends are doing. In other words, don't hide. They may provide valuable contacts for you if you're job-hunting or, more important, looking for a place to live. They've known you for years, so they can vouch for you.

Money Mistake: Your Kid Won't Leave Home

THE FIX: START THINKING LIKE A LANDLORD

This one's for parents: If you're complaining about Junior living in the basement, ask yourself if you've made it too easy for your kid to move back home. And if those are your kids at that restaurant I mentioned earlier, the ones who spend *your* extra money on fine dining, I have no sympathy for you. You've worked hard to make your home comfortable for your kids when they lived there—the pool, the video-game console, the massive TV in the family room, the cable, the high-speed wireless Internet. When they were in high school, yours was probably the home the kids all liked to hang out at, which was a source of pride for you and your spouse. When Junior chose the local community college because it was cheaper, and you let him come and go like the young adult he was, there were no questions and no rules. When he graduated and went looking for his own apartment, he had a hard time finding one with speakers by the pool and stainless-steel appliances. It just wasn't the same. So he gave up the search.

That was two years ago, and he's been comfortably ensconced in his—correction, I mean *your*—basement ever since. Meanwhile, you're still cooking and cleaning for a grown man. The truth is, your child is no longer a child, but an adult spoiled by the middle-class luxuries to which he (or she) has grown accustomed but has never earned.

First, congratulations. You raised a happy child. But never encouraging your kid to leave home, to find his or her own footing, is a dangerous thing. *You have to kick the kid out.* Plain and simple. You may think I'm being dramatic about this, but take a look at the statistics: According to *Forbes*, 15.8 million adult children were living with their parents at the end of 2012. A lot of those parents couldn't sell their houses when they wanted and needed to because their adult children were still hanging around, preventing them from liquidating the one asset they had set aside for a comfortable retirement. Timing is everything in the last few years leading to retirement; selling houses, downsizing, and transferring investments are tricky business. In other words, adult children living at home are interfering with crucial life and financial decisions parents have to make.

This is where it gets hard-core. But it's imperative that you understand you are helping your son or daughter in the long run. Your adult child needs to achieve self-sufficiency. Without that basic skill, I'm sorry, but your kid is not going to function well in the real world.

By letting your grown children overstay their welcome, you're teaching them they can quit jobs just because they feel like it. You're teaching them that other people will pick up after them, clean for them, cook for them, and cushion all their falls. You're teaching them that they're entitled to all the amenities without all the work. You're teaching them that if they pout, moan, or ignore a directive from you, it will go away. You're teaching them that life is too hard for them to handle on their own. Do you really want your child to learn those lessons?

Getting your deadbeat kid out of the basement is tough love at its harshest, but it's truly the only way. Consider this: It's mostly your fault, so you're going to have to suffer some discomfort as well—not just emotionally, but things will have to get a lot worse before they get a lot better. Trust me, in a little while, you'll look back on this time with gratitude. Even Junior will be grateful you did it. But now, this is ripping off a Band-Aid, times a thousand. Keep the deprivations purely financial. Put a dollar value on everything you give and he or she takes—from the toilet paper rolls that will begin to disappear to the gas tank that suddenly needs constant refilling. First thing you have to keep in mind is that this is not a child we're talking about. He or she is an adult, and should be treated as such.

Before you proceed, make sure you're not dealing with a young person suffering from depression, addiction, or mental illness of any kind. If you suspect you are, you must seek professional guidance. Don't hesitate. Also, if deep down you truly don't want your child to leave home, and in fact you enjoy both the company and having something to complain about, be honest with yourself. Just don't come crying to me in a few years when your kid is still living with you, along with a girlfriend and a baby or two, and your savings have been all but depleted.

But if you're sure you're dealing with a general lack of motivation, and you want that adult out of your house, keep reading for tips on what to do next.

10 Steps for Getting Your Kid Out of Your Basement

Your adult child needs you to be a tough parent. He or she just doesn't know it yet, and can't admit it. You, however, are doing nothing short of saving your financial, emotional, and marital health. Nothing is worth jeopardizing those things, certainly not your beloved child's material comfort. Follow these 10 steps to a tee—and in order—and you'll have your home back. And your kid will be on his or her financial feet in no time.

Step 1: **Start with a united front about tough love.** If you and your partner are not on the same page, the following measures will have a disastrous effect on the family.

Step 2: **Charge rent.** Set a market price for room and board. Charge that. No more, no less.

Step 3: **Set an end date.** Find a big calendar, and circle that date as the last one your child will spend living in your home. Don't negotiate that date, unless it's to move it forward. Give your adult son or daughter a maximum of three months to save enough money for first and last month's rent on an apartment that's not in your home.

Step 4: **Keep your car keys in your pocket.** Offer help with transportation only for appointments that have to do with finding a job or a place to live. That's it.

130

Step 5: Do not pay your son or daughter's bills. That means no subsidizing a cell phone, either, even if it's cheaper to keep it on a family plan.

Step 6: **Think like a landlord.** What do landlords do to kick out problematic tenants? They make life difficult for them. If your son or daughter is not obeying the rules or fails to show the appropriate signs of responsibility, cut the cable, wireless Internet, and central air. If you can control the hot water without affecting yourself and your spouse, cut that, too.

Step 7: **Cut out free meals, laundry, and cleaning services.** Your son or daughter should be paying for his or her own groceries and cleaning his or her own space and clothes (and yours).

Step 8: **Remind yourself that this is your house, purchased with your money that you earned doing your job.** It's at about this point that guilt can become monstrous. Remember, you're doing this for the good of your grown child.

Step 9: **Change the locks.** This means you may have to let your adult child into and out of the house at odd hours as he or she protests this inconvenience. Again, do it, cheerfully and respectfully, and mark off another day on the calendar.

Step 10: **If none of the above suggestions are helping, consider that you may have to move.** Your future downsizing plans will have to start sooner rather than later, and you need to put your financial well-being first. This isn't such a bad idea if the boomerang bird in question is the last to leave the nest. But if there are other young ones to consider, this is a difficult step to take. Depending on how adamant you are about getting your son or daughter to make this big step, this might be your last option.

CHAPTER 9

Young Love and Money

You worked like a dog through school. You held a part-time job, graduated, never moved back home—or if you did, your time there was short and strategic. Now you're on your own, tackling rent, your student loan (not car payments, because you're servicing debt and you live close to work, right? so you don't have a car), and you're about to start full-time employment in your first postgrad job. So why did you quit that bartending gig? You've been working there three, four nights a week all through school, but you could have gone down to one or two nights a week and still put in those forty hours as an office intern or an editorial assistant in the newsroom. It's great that you got that entry-level position at that ad agency, but it isn't going to pay much for a couple of years.

And it's during this time that you could begin to fall prey to a lot of unnecessary consumer spending. That's how it happens. Your income goes up a little, you suddenly feel flush. You stop putting money into your Secret 10 because you're suddenly buying shoes you can't really afford. And is that you throwing your credit card down on the table, treating your four friends to a dinner you can't afford? Why did you do that? You think you have money because you're finally earning it. Earning money is not the same thing as having money. *As long as you have consumer debt, you are not accumulating anything.*

I want to be very clear here. If your goal is to pay down that student debt as quickly as possible so you can begin to build a decent nest egg, or to save for that down payment on a house, it starts now. You saw the compound interest charts. You know that the more you sock away in your twenties, the more you'll have in your twilight years. To build that fortune, you have to lose the debt as soon as possible. So get your head around a fifty- to sixty-hour workweek—not forever, just for now. That is the only way you're going to get debt-free. I can't stress this enough.

We've learned that money equals time, so the more time you spend away from the clubs or the Internet or TV, and the more time you can spend working, the more money you're going to have. Another reason for working like a dog when you're young is that you're not going to be able to when you're old. And if you do it this way, you're not going to have to.

"But Uncle Kevin, what about balance? What about quality of life? Hobbies? Lounging around? Must everything always be about money?" Yes. Debt repayment is a critical skill. And if you master it when you're young, you're less likely to get into bigger, more problematic debts down the line. Here's the golden rule: *As long as you're paying a student loan, you're to continue to live like a student.* It's that simple. As long as there is debt associated with a previous lifestyle, you should be living according to that previous lifestyle. And here's another trick. As soon as that debt is paid, continue to live according to that previous lifestyle in order to get ahead. Up the amount you funnel into your Secret 10, to get even richer, but don't alter your lifestyle.

I'm going to let you in on a little secret. I have a home in Boston. It's an apartment in a historic brownstone, about one thousand square feet. I've owned and sold companies worth billions in the years since my wife and I first bought that place. My income has doubled, maybe even tripled since then. And guess what? I still own that little place. You might think it's nothing special, but my wife and I love it. It's the perfect size for us, and its layout is ideal for entertaining. It's "enough." As my income grew, our appetite for more stuff was relegated to a few big purchases, a summer home being one of them. And yes, I, too, bought a midlife-crisis car, and yes, even after I drove home and my wife said, "Oh, look, another bald asshole in a Porsche," I was still thrilled with the purchase. Because I put it in context: That car is a reward, a privilege for which I continue to pay dearly. But I don't lie to myself. It is not, and never will be, an investment.

Strategic investments, critical partnerships, and crucial financial timing led to the exponential growth of my wealth. But ultimately, it's this little-known and little-followed piece of advice that is the real key to growing wealth: Grow your money, not your lifestyle. Get into the habit early, kids, and maybe you'll earn yourself a Porsche one day, too. Maybe even before you lose your hair.

Money Mistake: You're Unsure Who Should Pay for What When Dating

THE FIX: TALK MONEY, THE SOONER THE BETTER

When should money begin to factor into a relationship? At what stage should you start to talk about money? Right from the get-go: the first date. Anytime there is a bill before you, or a movie ticket to pay for, is an opportunity to talk about money.

I have a son and a daughter. When I'm speaking to them together, I tell them this: Men should pay for the first date. It demonstrates that the guy is employed, is probably responsible, and can be relied upon to do the right thing. If Savannah dates a guy who proposes to split the bill on the first date, or lets her pay if she politely offers, I'm going to think he's a bozo and not worth her time, even if *she* asked *him* out. And I tell Trevor, "If you can't pay for a first date, you shouldn't be dating. You should be thinking about how to make more money."

However, when I speak to my kids separately, I give them conflicting advice, and in that overlap I hope they'll find their own way to navigate the financial aspects of dating. Here's what I mean. I tell Trevor that he should always pay when dating—I am an old-fashioned guy. Remember, I was raised by an elegant Mediterranean man who would never let my mother pay for a thing. On the flip side, I tell Savannah that, after the first date, she should offer to pay. In the overlap created by a man who assumes he should pay and a woman who offers, a couple will eventually map out their own financial blueprint, one that allows the partner who makes more to pay more and the one who makes less to make a contribution commensurate to his or her income.

This works for same-sex couples as well. Whoever initiates the date pays. After that, one offers to pay, the other to contribute. Once more, financial information is uncovered and shared. I suggest you employ rational ratios. Whoever makes more pays more. Period. You work out the specifics. Simply put, as the relationship progresses, each party should start to take turns paying for things, splitting expenses roughly equitable to what each earns, especially on things enjoyed as a couple, such as trips and meals. Using this method, you will naturally begin to know what each earns, how each spends, and what each person in the relationship expects in terms of money and spending.

Money Mistake: You're in Love, So You're Shacking Up

THE FIX: KNOW YOUR COMMON-LAW RIGHTS

The reasons for moving in together should be about money, too, not just love. After all, studies show that couples who live together before they get married aren't really inoculated against divorce. So lose the romantic idea that living together is practice for getting married, or that you'll make a better husband or wife because of it. If you're shacking up with your partner, it's important that you get a cohabitation agreement to avoid common financial dramas. Never assume that living together is "marriage lite."

A cohabitation agreement is like a *pre*-prenup, and can cost about $1,000 to $4,000. If things go south and you head to court, a cohabitation agreement can protect any assets that you bring to the arrangement and keep you from absorbing any of your partner's poor financial decisions. It can also lay out exactly who pays for what while you're living together, how money is managed, what shifts financially in the event of children, and more important, who inherits your money when you die. I say "more important" because child support falls under a different category, in that regardless of whether you're married, when you become a parent, you're financially obligated to the child. But if you are unmarried when you die, your money won't automatically go to your significant other.

For instance, let's say you and your partner have lived together for years, forgoing marriage because you both failed miserably at it the first time around. Let's also say you each have grown children from those failed marriages. If you do not put in writing that your partner should receive your money and your pension when you die, the surviving children have rights to it. And if they didn't like the man or woman you lived with all those years, they can stake claims on the house you shared when you were alive, forcing him or her out.

Also, beyond cohabitation agreements, there's never been a more important time to draw up a will than when you decide to live with someone. Many couples, especially ones without children living with them, skip this important paperwork, to their detriment. In the case of traumatic decisions like whether to let your partner continue on life support in the event of an accident or illness, your decisions can be overridden by any adult children of the ailing partner. And these are the kinds of decisions that can have a dire impact on everyone's financial future. So if you want control of your money, get everything in writing: who pays for what, who keeps what in the event of a breakup, and how things are to be dealt with when you die.

Make sure you hire a good lawyer, especially if you're bringing a lot of money into the partnership or your significant other is bringing a lot of debt. Here, you may have to reveal your Secret 10, but you certainly don't have to share it. By the way, if your potential partner is carrying a lot of debt, don't live together. I mean it. Stay in your separate abodes until you see that debt diminished.

You may have heard the "urban legend" that if you live together for seven years, you are common-law married. This is a pervasive misconception and is entirely untrue. In most states there is no way to form a common-law marriage, no matter how long you live with your partner. As of 2012, only nine states— Alabama, Colorado, Kansas, Rhode Island, South Carolina, Iowa, Montana, Oklahoma, and Texas—and the District of Columbia recognize common-law marriages. Five additional states have "grandfathered" common-law marriage: In other words, Georgia, Idaho, Ohio, Oklahoma, and Pennsylvania allow partnerships established before a certain date to be recognized as common-law. New Hampshire recognizes common-law marriage exclusively for purposes of probate, and Utah recognizes a marriage as common-law only if it has been validated by a court or administrative order.

STATE	REQUIREMENTS TO FORM A COMMON-LAW MARRIAGE
California	Not recognized.
Colorado	A common-law marriage may be established by proving cohabitation and a reputation of being married.
Florida	Not recognized.
Georgia	Only recognizes common-law marriages formed before January 1, 1997.
Kansas	For a man and woman to form a common-law marriage, they must: (1) have the mental capacity to marry; (2) agree to be married at the present time; and (3) represent to the public that they are married.

STATE	REQUIREMENTS TO FORM A COMMON-LAW MARRIAGE
Massachusetts	Not recognized.
New Hampshire	Common-law marriages are effective only at death.
New York	Not recognized.
Oklahoma	Only recognizes common-law marriages formed before November 1, 1998.
Pennsylvania	Law was amended to read: "No common-law marriage contracted after January 1, 2005, shall be valid."
Rhode Island	The requirements for a common-law marriage are (1) serious intent to be married and (2) conduct that leads to a reasonable belief in the community that the man and woman are married.
Texas	Texas calls it an "informal marriage" as opposed to common law. According to the Texas Family Code, an informal marriage can be established either by declaration (registering at the county courthouse without having a ceremony) or by meeting a three-pronged test showing evidence of (1) an agreement to be married; (2) cohabitation in Texas; and (3) representation to others that the parties are married.
Utah	Utah recognizes common-law marriage only if it arises out of a contract between two consenting parties who (1) are capable of giving consent; (2) are legally capable of entering a solemnized marriage; (3) have cohabited; (4) mutually assume marital rights, duties, and obligations; and (5) hold themselves out as and have acquired a uniform and general reputation as husband and wife.

As you can see, the elements of a common-law marriage vary slightly from state to state. The common elements are (1) cohabitation and (2) "holding out." "Holding out" is a fancy way of saying that the couple has announced to the world their roles as husband and wife—they file a joint federal income tax return, the woman may take the man's name, and so on. If you have part one without part two—two people who are cohabiting—it does not constitute a marriage.

As you might expect, all sorts of disputes can arise in a courtroom. For example, the two spouses may have had different intentions; they may also have made conflicting statements to friends, family, and community members. There are a million murky gray areas. To protect yourself from being mired in controversy and lengthy legal battles, I strongly urge you to put together an airtight cohabitation agreement and carefully study the laws in your state.

By the way, don't move in together because you think it'll better prepare you for marriage and diminish your chances of divorce. That's a myth. Study after study has shown that cohabitating couples are no more likely to stay together than those who move in after marriage. In fact, some studies say they're more likely to divorce, since cohabitating usually indicates the couple doesn't hold the institution of marriage in any real high esteem. So before you move in together, I suggest you do it only if you are indeed planning to get married.

One more caveat about this important financial decision. If living together eventually leads to marriage, you must stipulate that the cohabitation agreement is now a marriage agreement. Remember, once you say your vows, your cohabitation agreement is null and void. You're now married, and a very different set of financial worries kicks in.

10 Financial Questions to Ask Your Partner Before You Move In Together

Above all else, you have to get over your fear of talking about money as soon as possible. If you're about to join forces, combine your lives, and move in together, you need to know about your partner's relationship to money. That relationship will be joining you in yours, by the way. It isn't going to be just the two of you; it's the two of you plus the money (or debt) you bring to the relationship. Here's a list of questions you will want answers to before calling in the movers.

1. How much do you make a year (you'd be surprised at how few couples know this about each other!), and how do you imagine splitting our finances in the future?
2. How much debt do you have? How much of it is credit card debt?
3. Do you want kids? How many? (Yes, this is part of a financial decision.)
4. Have you ever been bankrupt or had a business that went under? How and why? How's your credit history now?
5. Do you borrow, or have you borrowed, money from family or friends?
6. Do you gamble or buy lottery tickets?
7. Do you have a pension or anything saved for retirement?
8. What about cars? Do you lease or own?
9. Do you have student loans? Are you making regular payments?
10. Describe your money style. Do you consider yourself a big spender or super frugal? What's more important to you: fancy holidays or paying down a mortgage?

These questions are just guidelines. I'm asking you to be as curious about your partner's financial history as you are about his or her familial, sexual, and educational background. If you have completely different financial styles and expectations, now is the time to find out, before you buy that condo together or walk down the aisle. What you're looking for is balance. Your potential partner is neither too cheap nor too generous. He or she doesn't throw away money, but also doesn't hoard it. Mostly, it's a good sign if having frank and honest financial discussions doesn't cause your partner to break out in hives and run in the opposite direction.

Dating is a time of discovery. You want to know if your potential partner is $200,000 in debt. You want to know what kind of financial future he or she envisions for him- or herself, because it's one you're going to share.

Part Three

MARRIAGE, MORTGAGE, AND CHILDREN

With Linda and the kids in Boston in the late 1990s when
The Learning Company was in full bloom.
(Property of Kevin O'Leary)

CHAPTER 10

Marriage and Money

It wasn't so long ago that marriage was only about money. Aligning financial interests, consolidating power between two families, rich dowries, and arable land—and not love, romance, and attraction—were the crucial components of a strong union. Our ancestors knew that when you marry, you marry each other's money, debts, and spending and saving habits.

I'm not advocating a return to arranged marriages, but if I have any goal in writing this book, it's to encourage open communication between couples about money, *before* they take the big plunge. Studies and polls consistently reveal that money problems ruin more relationships than infidelity. Yet many of these same polls and studies claim that people have a harder time talking about money problems than sex issues. Imagine if you discovered your partner-to-be had a history of gambling. You'd be right to cancel the wedding. So why would you head down the aisle with someone carrying $60,000 of credit card debt? Isn't that proof enough that your partner has gambled his or her future away? And if your fiancé(e) is having a torrid affair with money, it can be as insidious and destructive to your future marriage as an illicit affair.

Take the example of a couple I know, Sally and Frederick. Frederick is a hotshot commercial director who earns about $175,000 a year. As a high school English teacher, Sally earns less, about $65,000. They love each other very much, but they are about to embark upon the most debt-inducing journey they will ever go on in their lives: marriage.

Sally's happy because she thinks Frederick's making good cash. She envisions a comfortable future for herself, if not a downright luxurious one. Frederick's earning potential seems limitless because he's so talented. But here's what Sally doesn't know: Frederick has a $100,000 student loan, he's financed that fancy car he drives her around in, and he puts all those gourmet meals he treats her to on a credit card that carries a five-figure balance. Sally's marrying an *idea of Frederick,* because the real Frederick isn't showing through . . . yet.

Sally, on the other hand, with her modest teaching salary, no debt, and a condo with some healthy equity, actually has more worth than Frederick. In fact, *he* is lucky to be marrying *her!* And if Sally's not careful, those dreams of Costa Rican vacations and private school for the kids will morph into a stress-filled, debt-ridden, house-poor reality. Now, Sally is no dummy. Her gut is telling her something is not quite right, so she wants to talk to Frederick about money issues. But it seems that every time she raises the topic, Frederick gets angry. And whenever he gets angry, he goes out on a spending spree.

I know another couple who have a notoriously rocky relationship. Every time there's a problem, one of them heads to Neiman Marcus to rack up thousands of dollars in clothing expenses and the other one secretly buys high-end consumer products in retaliation. They use money as a way to communicate to each other what they feel they're worth. Expensive gifts are sometimes given in lieu of real intimacy and real communication.

Remember, the most important financial decision you'll ever make is who you'll marry. Not because of the money you both bring to the partnership, but because of the attitudes, outlook, honesty, career potential, and any number of other factors that determine compatibility. Divorce is expensive, so if you get any of this stuff wrong, you're looking at a potential depletion of wealth. Especially if your financial value systems don't line up with your partner's. No amount of love or sexual compatibility will make up for it. Your relationship is toast. This is why side-lining money discussions before marriage, *at any income level,* is dangerous. And prenuptial arrangements can go a long way toward exposing and sometimes amending these issues.

Don't forget that the average person gets married in his or her late twenties or early thirties. That's also the time they're carrying around a lot of debt, especially student loans, credit cards, and, potentially, a new mortgage. Blunt, honest money conversations should put you and your loved one on the same page financially. But the one thing you both need to align on is this: Prioritize paying down debt. You must both agree to delay big holidays or buying that boat—or even a house—until that debt is paid off. If you do that, your marriage will be on much stronger footing, and it'll likely stay there.

Money Mistake: You Don't Think You Need a Prenup

THE FIX: TREAT MARRIAGE LIKE A SMALL BUSINESS

According to the Bureau of Labor Statistics, only 49 percent of small businesses survive longer than five years. Those aren't great odds, which is why you would never get into business with someone on pure faith alone. When you enter into professional partnerships, you get everything in writing, before your small business even earns a dime.

So what other institution has an equally high failure rate after five years? Marriage. We all think we'll beat the odds, that we're different, special, that our love is uniquely suited to withstand the trials and tribulations of life. And I'm nothing if not a romantic at heart (believe it or not). That's why I love entrepreneurs so much—their stories, their gusto, their passion for a project, an idea, or a product. But I don't hand over a dime before performing thorough due diligence, without consulting trusted advisors, before getting every single detail of a business plan in writing. I go into every venture protecting myself against grand claims and probable changes of fortune. You'd be insane to do otherwise.

So why do so many people get married without doing the same kind of due diligence regarding their life partner? Why do many forgo a prenuptial agreement? Sometimes they say prenuptial agreements are for people who have a lot of assets to protect. Wrong. In this day and age, when so many women are outearning men and buying property before they are married, this piece of advice is particularly crucial: *Ladies, don't let him take you for an idiot. You must get a prenuptial agreement before you get married, regardless of your financial situation, especially if you own a business.* An ex-spouse, especially a vengeful one, can mire your business in the kind of legal drama that could completely bankrupt you. People will be unemployed, livelihoods will be destroyed, all because you were too shy to talk about money on a date. Think about it this way: If you can't talk about money, what other important subjects are off-limits? What to do in the event of illness? How you want to raise your kids? Whether you'd ever consider working and living abroad? Seriously, if you can't talk about money, how are you going to talk about topics that are even more sensitive?

Used to be, prenups were the purview of rich old men on their second or third wives, men who wanted to protect themselves against gold diggers after them only for their money. (I address this tricky topic in detail in Part Four.) But prenuptial agreements are not just for rich, older people anymore. Anyone coming into a relationship with any assets, any savings, any investments, however small, needs to get one. In fact, I can't think of a relationship that wouldn't benefit from financial clarity and protection. Remember, anything can happen. Even if both spouses come into a marriage with next to nothing, a windfall could occur later on that changes everything. So I want you to think of a prenup as *possible insurance against probable change.* You may never need it, but when the crap hits the fan, you're going to be very happy you had that difficult conversation.

Money Mistake: Prenup Is a Dirty Word

THE FIX: PRACTICE SAYING IT—OUT LOUD

Prenups are often criticized for being unromantic. That is because they are. They have nothing whatsoever to do with love—only with money. But there's an upside to introducing a prenup into your burgeoning relationship. You get to see what your partner's like during negotiations *before* you walk down the aisle. Contract talks are a fantastic vetting process. I've gone into a lot of boardrooms with levelheaded people, only to watch them turn into crazy people when things don't go their way. Instability is not a great trait in a business partner; it's never worse in a spouse or coparent.

Think of a prenup as a way to rationally consider the worst while you still really love your partner. You've been dating for six months, you haven't merged lives or made any outsized promises, but you are into each other; that's the time for hard conversations. And never apologize for bringing up the topic. Introduce it as a fact.

"Things are great, and I've never been happier. So it's hard to imagine this falling apart. But poo-poo happens. We both know that. And we'd be fools to think we're above the statistics. And I know I'm not marrying a fool. So let's talk money, honey. What do you expect to walk away with in the event I turn into Mr. Hyde?"

That's how I would do it. But you have to come up with your own dialogue, something that suits your style and reflects your concerns. Here are a few more things to keep in mind going forward:

Don't do it yourself. You can find all sorts of prenuptial agreement forms on the Internet with handy templates, but I don't recommend them, especially if you have assets totaling over $250,000. This isn't a time to scrimp. A good prenup will cost anywhere between $5,000 and $25,000, but it'll be the best money you've spent, because it'll save you many times that amount in the event of divorce.

Lawyer up. You will both need your own representation for a prenup, someone acting only in your interests and the interests of your money. Pick your lawyer based on your own personality preference. Want a keen negotiator, or someone who has the ability to gently coax? Also, don't just hire a lawyer; take his or her advice.

Keep it simple. Prenups can cover anything and everything, so a lot of people go crazy on the details. I suggest you avoid bogging down the document with issues like who keeps the salt-and-pepper-shaker collection or the set of prized golf clubs. Stick to divvying up large assets (who gets what), bills and debt (who pays what), property (who owns what), and estate (who inherits what). As I mentioned, child support falls under a different category, and even if you don't marry, you're required to pay it all the same in the case of a permanent separation. Pets should be addressed, especially any animals you adopt together. And don't forget vacation property, timeshares, and lake houses. I've heard the horror stories. A prized cottage in Cape Cod in one family for generations slips into the hands of the second wife or husband, even though the marriage lasted only a few years. Keep your requests simple and clear. It will save you a lot of money on lawyers later, and limit the opportunity for loopholes.

Say no to sunset clauses. This feature renders the prenup null and void after ten or fifteen years. A sunset clause gives a couple something to reach for, because they think they've made it past a certain hump and true love can then prevail. I do not recommend this. A lot of marriages explode in the twilight years. Love is treacherous at any time. That's not a bad thing; it makes you stay on your toes.

Keep legal contact to a bare minimum. Some of my friends are divorce lawyers. They make a lot of money filling out paperwork, but much of that income is earned answering teary phone calls and frantic emails from clients. Lawyers are good listeners. They're also going to bill you for every single tear, so hash it out over beers with your squash buddy, or commiserate with a friend. Call your lawyer only when you have an important legal question, and never, ever use your lawyer as a therapist. It's too expensive!

Money Mistake: You Think Marriage Means Mixing Finances

THE FIX: SLEEP TOGETHER, KEEP MONEY APART

Marriage means you can share a bed and split groceries, closet space, and chores, but it doesn't mean you have to merge your money. My mother and stepfather spent decades traveling around the world. In all that time, my mother grew her Secret 10—which wasn't a secret, really, but no one had any idea just how much was in her account until she passed away. George and my mother didn't merge money. They lived on George's income, and Georgette saved and invested hers. That was their choice, and it worked for them.

Before marriage, your conversations and negotiations, if conducted well, will have yielded crucial information about who keeps money safer. If your potential partner is bad with money, is carrying more debt than you, and spends too much, reconsider the merger. I wouldn't buy a company with that kind of financial profile.

But if you still want to proceed down the aisle, you can prevent disaster. You can still protect your money. Keep your Secret 10 yours and yours alone. Keep your own savings and investment accounts. Open a joint checking account in which you're each responsible to deposit a certain amount from your paychecks. Use that account to pay bills. Be separately responsible for your own debts, and jointly responsible for any debts incurred in the marriage. You're doing this to preempt disaster.

I'll add this bit of atypical advice: If my potential partner carried a lot of debt, I'd delay the wedding until the debt was gone, or consider marrying someone else. But if you're in a position to pay off your partner's debts, and you want to, don't make it a loan, make it a gift. This cuts down on resentment and introduces generosity into the relationship. It also reinforces the fact that this is a merger in every sense of the word. That said, if your partner responds to that gift by incurring more debt, double-check the prenup, rethink your plans, and call your lawyer.

Money Mistake: Damn the Risks, You're Getting Hitched

THE FIX: INVEST IN YOUR FUTURE, NOT IN YOUR WEDDING

Sometimes, when couples contemplating marriage take a cold hard look at their financial situation, they realize the potential financial drain a failed marriage can be, so they opt out. I encourage this, especially if you're not going to have kids. Let me repeat: *If you're not going to have kids, don't get married.* Live together, yes, commit for life, sure! Sign a cohabitation agreement, absolutely. But get married? No. I say this as a happily married man, so I'm not telling you to forgo the intimacy, security, and commitment that come from an exclusive relationship. I'm a big fan of all of that. I'm talking about the gamble that is marriage, and the expensive extricating process that is the average vicious divorce. (In fact, here's a brilliant rule of thumb: Don't marry anyone you'd be afraid to divorce.) And remember: Married people do not have a monopoly on soulmates. You don't always *find* your soulmate; as my wife says, you *become* soulmates after building something together over time, which should also include a healthy nest egg.

But maybe you're reading this and thinking the single lifestyle is not for you. After all, there are strong economic incentives to get hitched. It is more expensive to live alone. And studies do show that married couples who stay together build more wealth by the time they reach retirement.

So let's now assume you've had the hard financial discussions, signed a rock-solid prenup, decided you want kids, and therefore want to marry the love of your life. So why did you go and lose your financial mind over the wedding? Who are those four hundred people on the guest list? A horse-drawn carriage? A chocolate fountain? Seriously? And no one's even going to listen to that quartet playing during cocktails. No wonder the average cost of a North American wedding is $27,000. This figure never fails to stop me in my tracks. It varies by a couple of thousand dollars depending on where you live, but that, dear reader, is insane.

Beyond the colossal amount of money spent on weddings, it's the timing that kills me. When you're young—say, thirty years old or younger—it's the worst time in your life to throw $27,000 away on a single day. Remember, time is your greatest asset at that stage in life. People who overspend on their weddings are the same whiners who tell me afterward that they can't save enough money for a down payment on a house or pay off their credit card debt. Think about what else that money could do for you. If you invested a lump sum like that at the age of thirty and it earned only 3 percent a year, adding nothing to the principal, it would be worth more than $75,000 after thirty-five years. At 6 percent compounded interest, that same $27,000 would be worth more than $207,000 when you retire!

"Yeah, yeah, yeah," I can hear you saying. "But that's just the cost of doing things right." According to whom? According to the marital-industrial complex, the vicious cabal headed by the insidious wedding-planner industry, cosigned by celebrity rags that make people feel as if they have to treat their Big Day as the one time in their lives when they can act like they're famous? That's what's really going on at these monster weddings. Couples may think they're creating "lasting memories," but what they're really doing is creating a one-day spectacle to show off status they don't have. Look, unless you're a Kardashian and you've

Our wedding on March 17, 1990, with best man, John Suske, and maid of honor, Janet Cameron. We were broke! We did the whole wedding for $10,000. *(Nick Czudyjowycz, Einesport Productions)*

figured out how to get your wedding sponsored by major corporations, you can't afford doves and carriages. So get real, folks.

This is the part where I get to be more smug than usual: My wife and I spent $10,000 on our wedding, *including* a honeymoon in Barbados. True, we didn't have a lot of money at the time, and were I not a cheap bastard, we could have splurged a bit more. But Linda and I are cut from the same cloth. We agreed on a sane and sound prenup, and neither of us had any interest in wasting a lot of money on a big wedding. The piece of paper was more important to us than the size of the cake and the photo op.

How did we do it? We kept things simple. My best friend was my groomsman and Linda's maid of honor was her best friend. We had the reception in our home, a humble three-bedroom rowhouse with a small backyard. Linda and her friends decorated the place with balloons and fresh-cut flowers. Invitations were written on a DOS program and printed out at home. My wife made her own dress, and her grandparents drove her to the ceremony. I presented her with a simple gold band that cost $80—which, by the way, she still proudly wears today. We kept the guest list small. Friends who didn't make it onto the list offered to bartend so they could join the party. That was their gift to us, and their way of contributing to keeping the cost of the wedding low. We bought the alcohol at the liquor store. We didn't quite calculate properly and ran out of food, but it was nothing a phone call to a pizza place at midnight couldn't fix. Our one splurge was a night at a hotel before flying out on our honeymoon. That turned out to be our only waste of money. (The fire alarm went off just as we fell asleep. When it happened again an hour later, I ripped the alarm out of the ceiling.)

Perhaps you're thinking our wedding sounds like it was nothing special. You're wrong about that. The focus was exactly

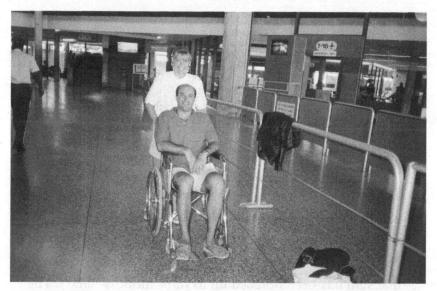

I herniated my L4 and L5 discs on our honeymoon, and could not walk for eight days. It made me realize the value of having some emergency cash.
(Property of Kevin O'Leary)

where we wanted it to be: on us, our close friends and family, and our commitment to each other. It was a perfect wedding for many reasons, but mostly because we didn't drain our savings and enter marriage in debt. Remember this if you're planning a wedding: Memories are created by people, not products.

Get Hitched and Stay Rich: 10 Ways to Minimize Wedding-Spending Madness

Okay, so you've hired me, Mr. Wonderful, the frugal wedding planner. Lucky for you—unlike those expensive busybodies running around with Bluetooth devices, I'm offering my wedding-planning services for free. My wedding-planner business is called

Love Don't Cost a Dime, Inc. My goal: to force you to scrutinize every single cost, to reevaluate every expensive so-called tradition, and to find the cheapest possible way to get hitched and stay rich.

My approach is a little tongue-in-cheek, but the message is clear: Don't let matrimonial madness consume you.

1. **Forgo the engagement ring.** Diamond companies are almost as smart as banks—De Beers in particular. In the 1940s, it was the first company to market the idea that a guy has to spend a couple months' salary on the engagement ring. Why? No reason. It's just a brilliant marketing ploy. Mysteriously, that sum has been notched up to three months' salary. The genius idea has become that if your guy buys you a crappy ring, he's not valuing the relationship as much as he should. I'm telling you, the engagement ring racket is a load of crap. It's a made-up concept. Don't fall for it.

   Want to be romantic? Tell your bride she'll get a very nice ring on your tenth anniversary, if your marriage survives that long. Buy your hubby a set of golf clubs or cuff links on your fifth. That's when it'll really mean something, and, if you've planned wisely, you'll have the cash to splurge and pay in full. Meanwhile, a simple wedding band should suffice. Nothing says romance like wisely investing the money you would have blown on an engagement ring.
   Savings: $1,000–$10,000.

2. **Bands at weddings suck.** Go with a DJ at your wedding, not a live band. Why? Wedding bands suck. Worse, they cost a lot more than a talented DJ, or your music-savvy

cousin. And please have mercy and ban the quartet playing near the ice sculpture. A quartet just forces drunk people to talk louder. Also, about your ice sculpture: If I see it at your wedding, I'll put a blowtorch to it. There is no greater waste than spending thousands of dollars you can't afford on frozen, Cupid-shaped water.

   Savings: $1,000–$5,000.

3. **Skip the honeymoon.** Who says you have to go on a honeymoon? Again, this is an expense that, when analyzed, isn't entirely necessary. Go only if you have the money to do so. But remember, you pay a premium for the honeymoon packages and suites, because travel agents and hotels know that your flight times are often fixed, and you're going to be arriving in a "bliss bubble" and therefore be vulnerable to all sorts of add-ons during your special time. Forgo the champagne baths and double massages. Say no to chocolate spa treatments and romantic boat cruises. Stay away from any packages using the term "honeymoon." And don't plan to leave right after the ceremony. Be flexible with your times and suss out the deals. Instead of a honeymoon, cash in a few vacation days and lounge around the house. Call *that* your honeymoon. Ask friends with a lake house to let you have it for a few days. Then use the honeymoon money to put a down payment on your first home.

   Savings: $1,000–$10,000-plus.

4. **No flowers.** Flower arrangements at weddings are a tragic waste of money. People spend a fortune picking them out, arranging them perfectly, sticking them in bowls, wrapping

ribbons around the vases, transporting them to the hall, then *throwing them in the garbage a few hours later*. Try this handy decorating tip from Mr. Wonderful. Take $5,000 worth of $20 bills, which is an amount lots of people budget for flowers. Fold them into pretty origami roses. Put them on sticks. Arrange them in vases. At the end of the night, instruct each wedding table to light the money on fire. This would be cheaper than flowers and would save on composting.

Savings: $1,000–$5,000-plus.

5. **Get married on a Monday.** Okay. Maybe not a Monday, but definitely don't get married on a Saturday, because everything's at a premium on a Saturday. You'll pay extra for parking for the limo, for the hall, and for that last-minute seamstress session. Get married on a Thursday or Friday night. Get married in the winter. Be a little different. A weekday wedding will also force your binge-drinking cousin (who shouldn't be invited anyway—see below) to go easy on the bottle. Take the next day off work, though. Live a little.

Savings: $2,000–$5,000.

6. **Keep the guest list minimal.** Weddings are priced by the head, so you have to be like the doorman at the hottest club in town. Who really gets onto the list? Immediate family, sure. Aunts and uncles? Maybe. Coworkers? Depends. Friends? That's when things get problematic. Scan that list with a vicious eye. You're an accountant first, a blushing bride later. If you've known these friends for five, ten years, maybe that's your cutoff. Maybe you invite only people

who are friends with both you and your betrothed. Pay particular attention to cousins. Do you really care if they're at your wedding? Another cost saved.

Savings: $2,000–$10,000-plus.

7. **Don't scrimp on the booze.** This is the only place you don't want to cut costs. Booze should flow from the minute your guests arrive until the minute you insist on pouring them into a cab. It may seem counterintuitive and "off message," but I promise you this: When people have a couple of drinks, they're less picky. They likely won't notice the crappy DJ, the balloons in lieu of flowers, or the fact that it's all taking place on Thursday night.

Savings: None.

8. **Bring back money rituals.** Italians have it right. I like how they shop, and I like how they celebrate big events with cold hard cash. Had a baby? Here's some money. Communion time? Whom do I make this check out to? Getting married? Here's a fat envelope for the basket. It's always about money. Unlike knickknacks, baubles, and trinkets, money adds pageantry and permanence to any occasion. When you give money, you're saying, "Here, I'm investing in your love, your goals, your future. I want prosperity for you. Let me contribute." Giving someone a blender just says, "I don't know you very well, but good luck."

Savings: $3,000–$10,000-plus.

9. **Ban the bridesmaids.** Skip the wedding party. Having just a maid of honor and a best man means they won't have to

spend a lot of money on their own outfits. And you won't have to blow a wad on gifts thanking them for going broke on behalf of your wedding. It'll also cause fewer fights and headaches, as ten bridesmaids means picking ten dresses everyone likes and looks good in, coordinating ten multiple fittings, and corralling everyone for the pricey photo sessions.

Savings: $5000-plus.

10. **Stay married.** It's the best way to save money. I have friends who are on their third or fourth marriage. Every time they walk down the aisle, they say they've found "the one," and don't they have the right to be happy? A few years later, life's not happier with the new wife. It's just different. Look, I'm not against love, but if you're getting married three or four times, you might want to consider that you're bad at being married. That's okay. I'm sure you have other talents. There's a direct comparison to entrepreneurs who drive every business they helm into the ground. Maybe they're better off getting a job than running a company.

My wife and I have been through a lot in our twenty-plus years together. There have been ups and downs and some very close calls. But we make it work. Why? For me, it always comes down to this: Linda is the only woman in the world I know, with complete, 100 percent certainty, loves me for exactly who I am. I know this because she married me when I had nothing. That's love.

Savings: Incalculable.

CHAPTER 11

House Poor, House Rich

So you skipped my advice and got married anyway. But you did sign a solid prenup, didn't blow a wad of money on the wedding, and now you're happily married. And because you've made money a primary concern, your first fights actually aren't *about* money. They're about space—closet space, and who gets the one parking spot in the winter. You're probably still living in the same apartment you lived in when you were dating. But now you're thinking of starting a family. So wedding talk is soon replaced by talk of open houses, floor plans, and mortgages.

Home ownership is a powerful lure, and we live in a real-estate obsessed world. Alongside gold, homes are one of the few investments I have made in my life that do not pay dividends. I own my fair share of property, which has tended to increase in value over time. But while a home is an important investment in anyone's portfolio, it must be seen in a different category from most investments. It may or may not appreciate in value rapidly, so it should be considered a safety net, not your primary investment. Once paid for, your home becomes an asset you can rely on, no matter what is happening in the world around you. Still, there are many things to consider before you take that big first step toward getting a mortgage.

Fact is, home ownership often forces you to break a lot of sound investment rules. You're borrowing most of the money from the bank, so you're highly leveraged. You're illiquid, so if you need cash fast, you can't just sell a house—it's a process that often takes months and months, and takes a big bite out of your bottom line. And because of the sheer cost of an average house in an average American city, your home is your greatest asset and your biggest investment, so your portfolio is far from balanced. When you put a disproportionate percentage of your investments into one asset class, it can be a recipe for disaster. And yet, it's hard to argue with people who believe that buying a home is the next logical step in building wealth.

Historically, house prices have tracked inflation, meaning that a dollar invested in your home today will still be worth a dollar when your great-grandchildren inherit it. The market may boom or bust, the Eurozone may disintegrate, oil may shoot through the roof, but once you pay off your mortgage, you have the security of knowing that the land and property is yours. But remember: Mortgages are banks' number-one moneymakers, which is why they're often easy to get—and hard to get out of. And in the United States at least, a mortgage is not a huge risk to a bank. Quite the opposite. It's the beginning of a long love affair. Once banks have that long-term relationship with you, they can sell you all sorts of other things: insurance, lines of credit, and credit cards. They now have a tremendous amount of information about you. They know where you live, where you work, and how much you make. And if anything goes wrong, the bank owns your home.

Consider the recent mortgage crisis. There are a lot of murky factors on Wall Street that led to that tragic crash, but at the start of this dilemma, lenders were selling the dream of financial freedom through real estate, and overleveraged buyers with stars in their eyes were given way too much mortgage, too soon. Too many people entered the real estate market overextended and overly ambitious about what they could really afford. And banks were only too eager to lend them the money. Buyers were lulled by subprime mortgages, which had them paying virtually nothing on the principal for most of the early portion of the mortgage, at very low interest rates. When those rates went up, drastically, many could no longer afford the payments, and by the time they tried to sell their houses, they found they had built little to no equity. When it all came tumbling down, homes across the country lost trillions of dollars in value. Many were abandoned to the same banks that provided the subprime mortgages. Worse, unsellable houses meant a less mobile workforce, so as jobs also disappeared, millions of people were stranded. It takes a long time to recover from that kind of tragedy.

Money Mistake: You Don't Know If You're Ready to Buy a House

THE FIX: STABILITY IS AS IMPORTANT AS AFFORDABILITY

Banks have their own criteria for mortgage qualification, and they change from bank to bank. But laws governing the banks change, too, and there's been a steady parade of new laws and regulations ever since the housing bubble burst. In the years leading up to 2008, lenders were offering subprime mortgages to unqualified homeowners—people with bad credit and a lack of steady income. This resulted in a catastrophic collapse of the housing market, which caused the financial quagmire we're still digging out of today.

Five years and a $9.7 trillion bailout later, a number of laws have been passed to prevent a future housing crisis. As recently as January 2013, the Consumer Financial Protection Bureau revealed new rules regarding what kind of loans banks can offer and to whom. The Ability-to-Repay and Qualified Mortgage rule protects borrowers from mortgages they can't afford, which in turn protects lenders from being sued for granting mortgages they never should have granted. In a post-housing-bubble industry largely dominated by Fannie Mae, Freddie Mac, and such government agencies as the Federal Housing Administration, the rule is meant to provide the legal framework for private lenders to service mortgages with increased confidence and protection.

The rule creates a new standard mortgage in the United States called a "qualified mortgage." Interest-only loans, loans carrying balloon payments, and loans with terms of more than thirty years will no longer be considered "qualified." And if a would-be borrower's total debts equal or exceed 43 percent of his or her monthly gross income, no mortgage for that person. But astonishingly, the new rules make no mention of down payments. When the FHA continues to offer home loans for 3.5 percent down, no wonder the housing market remains a slippery slope!

Though conventional mortgages require a down payment of 20 percent, home buyers can easily secure a smaller down payment by obtaining private mortgage insurance. Because nothing is free where banks are concerned, PMI curtails a hefty fee for the homeowner. Depending on your credit rating and the length of your loan, it typically costs around 0.5 to 1 percent of your mortgage balance each year.

I'm far more conservative than the bank or the government. I like to see a down payment of 20 to 25 percent, even on a lower-priced home. But the additional cost of private mortgage insurance is a good cutoff. If you can't put down 20 percent and avoid that fee, you probably can't afford to buy a house. If you *do* buy that house, count on being house poor. PMI protects the bank in the event that you default. That means if you're putting only 15 percent down on a $500,000 home, you're throwing $4,250 away on private mortgage insurance—and that's just the first year. Dumb. Don't do that. Rent instead, and save until you've got your 20 percent together.

Another good rule of thumb is not to buy a house that'll sap more than 25 percent of your income, or up to 30 percent in cities where homes are above average in price. Sure, the Ability-to-Pay and Qualified Mortgage rule says 43 percent, but that's way too high for my blood. Consider Sam and Lila, whose combined yearly income is $100,000. Their mortgage payments, tax, upkeep, and insurance shouldn't add up to more than $25,000 a year. If they live in Minneapolis, that would be a realistic ratio. But if they live in San Francisco, where the average cost of a single-family home is $780,000, or New York City, where the average home costs $1,020,000, they'd be spending anywhere from 45 to 60 percent of their household income just on their home.

More than almost any other financial decision you make, a mortgage will determine your quality of life for years to come. When you're spending 60 percent of your monthly salary on your home, the quality of your life suffers. And many people pay right to the level they can afford. In other words, they stretch, and their ambition exceeds their ability to afford it. They become "house poor," where every extra dollar, and all their extra time, go into servicing their one big asset. They eat Lean Cuisine in front of the TV because they can't afford to go out or even buy real food at the grocery store. Their kids' education funds get cashed in early because they need to fix the roof. These are all-too-common scenarios, and they represent a recipe for a miserable life. You didn't buy a house to be one leaky roof, one fallen tree, or one boiler mishap away from disaster.

Maybe you aren't like that Minneapolis real estate mogul who went to war on his mortgage and made a fortune. Maybe you just want your home to be a stable place to raise your family, while it accumulates value and equity over time. But regardless, your mortgage is debt. I get that the need to own a home is primal, the nesting urge we may have inherited from our ancestors. But our ancestors enjoyed much cheaper housing. If you're not the type to spend every waking hour paying down that mortgage, if priority one from the minute you sign those bank papers isn't to get to a place where you never have to deal with banks again, then you're not cut out to be a homeowner.

Where affordability is a cold hard number, mobility erodes equity, because every time you buy and sell a house, you're losing at least 12 percent of its value to closing costs, real estate fees, and land transfer taxes. Then there's the cost of moving and furnishing the new place. So your home has to appreciate that much at least during the time you own it to make the purchase and sale worth it. That doesn't happen in a year or two. That takes a while. Not everybody lives in a hot real estate market. Bottom line is that for many people, a home is a *good long-term bet, not a short-term investment*. So don't buy a home too early, or one that's too big, and never sell it too soon.

Here's a typical scenario. Angela buys that one-bedroom box in the sky because she wants that "pride of ownership" feeling. A year later, she meets Scott, who's "the one." They decide to buy their own place. Angela sells her condo for more than what she bought it for, but remember, she also subtracts 12 percent for purchasing and selling costs. So she ends up with $50,000 in equity. Scott and Angela find a three-bedroom townhouse. She and Scott split the $50,000 down payment. They buy the house, move in, and spend another $25,000 each on renos and furnishing. Now Angela's tapped out. Six months later, they break up. Scott offers to buy her out for $30,000. They didn't sign a cohabitation agreement and they weren't married. Poor Angela. She's lost a big chunk of equity because she didn't act prudently from the beginning. Both Angela and Scott should have tested their relationship for several years before taking on such a huge financial responsibility. Instead, they jumped ahead to a three-bedroom house before making sure the relationship was going to last. Too much dreaming, not enough reality equal money down the drain. So beyond affordability, it's lack of stability—the moving, the flip-flopping, and the uncertainty inherent in our youth—that does people in financially.

Money Mistake: You Think Homeownership Is the Only Option

THE FIX: RENT, DON'T BUY

Before I dissect what kind of mortgage to get and how to pay it off faster, I want to touch on a little-discussed home option: renting. Because one way to be mortgage-free forever is to never buy a house to begin with. Or to sell at the right time and rent thereafter. Bear with me. This is often a tough nut to swallow. But here's the truth: *If you don't have the fortitude to cope with the insatiable costs of a house, you're better off renting.* It's not for everyone, but renting makes good financial sense for a lot of people. If you have a lot of debt, for instance, renting might be a better option. You would think the checks and balances of the loan application would render folks carrying big debt ineligible for a mortgage, but you'd be wrong. Banks want the business, and if you are making debt payments on time, they will consider you for a mortgage. But don't kid yourself. A house is a hotbed of the unexpected. If you have debt, you should rent.

If you're in your twenties, your primary concerns should be eliminating any debt, paying off student loans, and finding a great-paying job. That means staying mobile. You have to go where the jobs are. Buying a house keeps you locked in one location, and big fees and taxes are attached to liquidating that asset. And I know you just said you need more space, but money problems are love killers. Nothing will end the honeymoon sooner than a leaky roof that has to be paid for with a credit card because the line of credit was used to pay for the wedding. Just continue to rent until a year or two after you have kids. And definitely wait until the honeymoon's *really* over so you have a better idea how each of you handles money.

What kills me the most is when people who can't change a washer on a faucet, let alone a lightbulb, want to take on the care and maintenance of an old, crumbly fixer-upper. Contractors and repair people make a fortune off people like that. If you are chronically useless around the house and don't plan to change, don't buy a house. And certainly, if you're a freelancer, an artist, or you work contract to contract, you've got enough stress in your life. I have a lot of respect for artists and risk-takers, people who are giving their all to make it in their chosen field. Sometimes, a moment of great success, like a big advance on a book or a hit single, will finally yield enough money to allow you to make that healthy down payment on a house. Proceed with caution. You're in a business that is as moody as the markets. A good year doesn't mean you can afford a house. A few good years might. Concentrate on making it big before buying. When that happens, you can buy a house outright—no mortgage, no stress, no problem. Until then, spend that extra money on guitars, getting better headshots, or flying to those auditions in L.A.

With everything we know about home ownership, the pitfalls and potential financial hazards, I'm still baffled that renting carries with it such an unfair stigma. To be a tenant implies that you're transient, unreliable, and unstable. Yet in Switzerland, one of the richest countries in the world, almost two-thirds of the population rents rather than buys. And they enjoy various incentives, such as tax breaks and other deductibles, that the U.S. government offers only to homeowners.

You rent to save on expenses. You rent to avoid the stress of home ownership. Owning a home is a part-time job. Think of your rent money as the cost of all the time you aren't spending raking leaves and shoveling snow or dealing with the raccoons in the attic. You rent because it's predictable. You know your monthly nut. There are strident laws protecting you from casual eviction or greedy landlords, and the cost of moving is just a truck and two guys—no lawyers or real estate agents need to be involved.

I can hear a number of you saying, "But Uncle Kevin, I've always been told that investing in real estate is the only way to build wealth." Here's a terrific compromise for those of you who want the benefit of investing in real estate without all of its attendant headaches: Invest in REITs—real estate investment trusts. REITs are like mutual funds—baskets of assets, except that they carry real estate investments only. As with mutual funds, you invest collectively and reap the profits proportionate to your investment. It's a way to own property without being a landlord, paying property taxes, dealing with repairs and upkeep, or paying the 12 percent in taxes and real estate fees every time you want to sell your property. REITs can involve commercial or residential properties, condos, strip malls, storage facilities, or farms. I suggest you hire a qualified financial advisor to help you select the REITs you want to invest in.

To rent or to buy is a personal choice. But if you do decide to rent, here is some simple math to show that, while owning often builds equity, it also comes at a steep cost, one that is sometimes equal to the cost of renting.

You have $100,000. Do you rent or do you buy?

Let's say you buy a two-bedroom condo for $350,000. You use that $100,000 as your down payment. That means paying $1,400 a month on a $250,000 mortgage at 4 percent interest. On top of your mortgage payments, you also pay $500 a month in condo fees, $200 in utilities, $200 a month in taxes, and $50 a month in insurance.

Here is your total output every month to own a condo, keeping in mind that your mortgage payments, at least for the first few years, are largely servicing the interest, not the principal: $2,350, much of it in taxes, utilities, and fees.

Over a twenty-five-year period, that mortgage might cost you about $145,000 in interest, assuming your rate never goes up or down. So yes, at the end of twenty-five years, you'll have built equity, and the value of your condo may have more than doubled, maybe even tripled. But so, too, will your taxes and fees. Not to mention the two, maybe three, renovations you'll have done on the condo; the new floors ten years in, the new bathroom at fifteen, and the complete overhaul of the kitchen at twenty.

So let's say at the end of twenty-five years, your $350,000 condo is worth $750,000. Good investment. But let's subtract just the $145,000 in interest and, say, $100,000 in renos, and the real value is $505,000. That doesn't include the years of fees and taxes, but that's the price of home ownership.

The goal, if you choose to rent, is to find not only a place that's cheaper, but one that allows you to invest the difference between what you're paying in rent and what your output would be *if you had carried that $2,350 in monthly payments.*

Let's say you're lucky and find a one-bedroom with a den, utilities included, for $1,600 a month (which goes up about 2 percent every year). Now, instead of putting that $100,000 toward a down payment, you save and invest it. Let's also say you'll be ambitious, and on top of the initial $100,000, you'll invest another $750 a month, the difference between what it would have cost you to own at $2,350 per month in mortgage payments and the $1,600 in rent. Over the course of twenty-five years, your investments enjoy an average 4 percent return. At the end of that period, you will have earned almost $700,000, a bit more than the equity you built in the condo, without the headaches and worry that come with owning a home. Mind you, those rewards are offset by the fact that every month, your rent helped build your landlord's equity, not yours. But if your rent payments fall in the same ballpark as a condo owner's fees and taxes, as well as increases to both, then you can see that with either option you're paying out money you'll never see again.

As a homeowner, you'll probably always come out ahead financially. But not by as much as people often think. And that victory comes at a cost that some people aren't willing to pay. If you're a savvy investor and a dedicated saver, renting can be a more suitable option than home ownership.

Money Mistake: You Don't Know What Kind of Mortgage to Get

THE FIX: CHOOSE PREDICTABILITY OVER VARIABILITY

I don't like variables of any kind. More financial mistakes are made when your future is a mystery. If you opt for a low-interest variable mortgage that has you paying only $1,000 a month, you're lulled into thinking that you can afford a pricey European vacation because your mortgage payments are so low. Suddenly, when rates shoot up—and they will—you're now paying $300 more per month on your mortgage. Meanwhile, you had put that vacation on a line of credit, for which you calculated you'd be paying $400 a month for two years. Then you almost miss a mortgage payment, but you think to transfer a bit of money from your credit card to your checking account, just to cover the line of credit—but just this one time. Then it happens: You get laid off. This is how debt begins. Now your manageable $1,000-a-month mortgage payment has almost doubled to include debts incurred because you didn't make the requisite financial adjustments. Specifically, you kept spending as if your mortgage would never go up. This was the story heard over and over again during the housing crisis. It always starts small—a missed payment or two coupled with a big purchase that was ill timed. Then comes the unforeseen job loss. Soon, the same bank that convinced you to opt for that low-interest variable mortgage owns your house. Too often, people who opt for a less-expensive variable mortgage plan forget that things may change.

Money Mistake: You Aren't Maximizing Your Mortgage Payments

THE FIX: GET A FIXED MORTGAGE THAT LETS YOU PAY DOWN PRINCIPAL

So you found your dream house, you've negotiated an excellent rate with the bank, and you've booked the movers. Next on the homeowner's agenda is to go to war on your mortgage. You must think like that old millionaire in Minneapolis.

As an investment philosophy, I like predictability. I also like simplicity. That's why I say *paying off your mortgage is the best investment you could ever make.* I'll break it down like this. In 2013, the average mortgage rate in this country was roughly 3.67 percent. Very few investments can *guarantee* that return. I mean *guarantee.* And in the last few volatile years, average investors took a serious hit in their portfolio. In other words, they lost money on the markets, while their homes slowly but steadily appreciated in value. In 2012, home values were appreciating at robust monthly growth rates, reaching the highest rate of appreciation since 2005. By the end of 2013, national home values are expected to appreciate by 1.1 percent, with substantially higher growth in some areas—*Forbes* predicts 9.9 percent appreciation in Phoenix and 6.1 percent in Miami.

Now keep in mind these are just predictions, and there have

certainly been bad years as well. But home values tend to go up alongside inflation, which protects your money over the long term. Saying all that, by paying down your mortgage, you are almost guaranteed a positive return. But if there's one piece of advice you should take from this chapter, it's this: *There is no scenario in which you will be guaranteed a higher return on your investment than if you pay down your mortgage.* You are 100 percent guaranteed a return on investment. What other investment can you make that will guarantee that? So make eliminating your mortgage second on your list of things to do to retire richer. Eliminating debt is still number one.

Here's my favorite mortgage model in an economic environment in which interest rates are likely to rise: a five-year fixed-rate mortgage, but one that allows you to tackle a good chunk of the principal (up to 20 percent every year) without a penalty. You will save boatloads of money. You don't need a longer mortgage, because most people don't stay in their first homes for more than five years anyway. During the course of your mortgage, you're going to save as much as you can to hit your target, whatever maximum principal the mortgage allows you to pay down. That's your goal. Will you do it? Maybe, maybe not, but what a perfect way to monitor spending. You will begin to tell yourself *every dime not spent paying down that mortgage had better matter.* Also, structure your mortgage payments so they're lined up with your paycheck and are automatically withdrawn.

I also recommend that you make biweekly payments. It will have you making an extra mortgage payment every year without even feeling it, and it could shave more than three years off the average twenty-five-year mortgage, saving you thousands in the long run. If you're currently making monthly payments, switching to biweekly is just a phone call away. And it's usually free.

You aren't renegotiating your mortgage, after all, just changing the way you pay it.

How will you pay down that principal? You will apply every windfall to your mortgage. That means raises, tax returns, bonuses, inheritances—all of it goes to paying down the maximum principal allowed. And finally, round up your payments. I like lots of zeros (when they come after other big digits, of course). Are you paying a mortgage of $766 every two weeks? Why not make it an even $800? It seems like a simple thing to do, but over time, this little trick will have a huge impact on your overall savings. It just takes a phone call to your bank.

Money Mistake: You Think Home Renovation Is an Investment

THE FIX: RENOVATE STRATEGICALLY

I can't mention home ownership without addressing the number-one reason people struggle to pay down their mortgages: badly planned, poorly timed renovations. Americans love to renovate. Home renovation is one of the fastest-growing industries in the market. In 1999, it was a $180 billion industry. In 2007, it reached a peak of $326 billion. Home renovation dipped after the housing crisis, but today it is still a thriving $279 billion industry. Even more remarkable: Remodeling accounts for about 70 percent of residential spending. Partly, this is because houses are expensive, so people are hunkering down and improving their own nests and castles. But high prices also mean lots of speculation. People are renovating and flipping homes in the hope of making a buck on the margins. That's a risky gambit.

So much can go wrong, from unscrupulous contractors to unexpected surprises, falling housing prices, and insurance nightmares that eat into your costs. That said, in a tough economy, renovating is sometimes a good way to increase the value of your one big investment. A few small improvements can increase the value when it comes time to sell.

On the pages that follow are a few ways to ensure your renovations result in a good investment.

10 Ways to Renovate Smarter

1. **Don't just get quotes.** Yes, you want to get some prices, but don't skip the references. It's not enough to do a cost comparison, because those costs invariably go up. (Count on paying at least 20 percent over the budget, by the way.) You need to know how close that contractor generally comes to the quote, and the only way to know that is by getting the numbers of the last few clients. Read reviews of potential contractors and companies you're thinking of hiring on sites that review contractors and other home improvement services. This is the purest form of word of mouth available.

2. **Do some, not all, of it yourself.** Leave the plumbing and electrical to the pros, even if you have the skills, because doing it yourself could lead to insurance problems down the line. But why not paint the walls yourself? Slap on some overalls and buy good-quality paint and brushes. You cut about 20 percent off your budget by doing the messy, fussy part of the renovation yourself.

3. **Do your own shopping.** A lot of contractors charge by the hour, and a lot of those hours are spent standing in line at IKEA or Home Depot. Get a list on a daily or weekly basis from your contractor for materials you don't need a contractor's discount to purchase. Spend your evenings picking up those small items, whatever fits in your car—trim paint, hinges, grout. And make sure you hire someone who's okay with your doing some of the shopping. Many contractors don't like it because they make a good chunk of money staying on the clock as long as possible.

4. **Apply for the proper permits.** You think it's nobody's business that you're putting a kitchen in your basement so that you can earn a little income renting it out? Think again. Licensing and permitting are a city's way of earning a steady stream of revenue. Also, in the event of a fire or a mishap, illegal renovations might render your insurance claim null and void. So you may be wasting money insuring your home if you have an illegal basement apartment. Just make sure, if you open a permit, that the work is completed and an inspector signs off on it. There's nothing worse than trying to sell a home with an open permit. Before you can close the sale, you must complete the scope of the work outlined in the original permit, which could mean thousands of dollars in unexpected costs. If you don't want to complete that work, have the drawings redone, then refile for a new permit.

5. **Pick your rooms.** It's nice to have a walk-in closet, skylights, and a gym in the basement, but for a guaranteed return

on your renovation investment, the only certainties are an updated kitchen and a sparkling bathroom. The other big draw is a family room on the main floor, and a bathroom off the master bedroom. Anything else on your wish list should wait or be axed. This is how people get into financial trouble—by over-renovating and committing to projects that don't add value to the home, but add only debt.

6. **Buy smarter.** When it comes to building materials, your contractor should enjoy a discount of as much as 20 percent from affiliated stores off the prices of all materials. But where possible, skip retail altogether. Look for leftover or discontinued stock for items like sinks and flooring. Attend auctions, and scour online stores for unique materials that might come at a lower cost. Then buy, ship, and store until you're ready to use them.

7. **Don't skip the plans.** A lot of contractors will tell you that you don't need architectural plans to do your renovation. And in some cases, you don't. But if you're moving fixtures, tearing down walls, or relocating the toilet or any electrical work, then spend the money on an architect. They generally charge between 10 and 20 percent of the overall budget, but it's well worth it to avoid getting into bigger problems later. Finding out in the middle of construction that a fridge doesn't fit or there's not enough counter space in the kitchen is a budgetary nightmare. Architects not only help you visualize the finished project; they help foresee potentially expensive problems so you can avoid them.

8. **If you have to borrow, you can't afford a reno.** In the last few years, the single biggest expense people have put on a line of credit is home renovation. Blame the flood of DIY channels, home improvement, and real estate programs, but banks have largely financed American renovation fever, at an alarming rate. Resist the temptation to go into huge debt to renovate your home. The interest you'll pay over the years of servicing that debt will overshadow the gains you make with the renovation.

9. **Don't over-renovate.** It's called overcapitalizing when you spend more money on your house than the margin you'll reap when you sell it. A colleague of mine once bought a historic rowhouse. Hers was in the middle of two other units. The outside units had upstairs bedrooms because the owners could simply insert a window on the side of each house. After adding a kitchen on the main floor and a basement suite, my colleague looked into adding a second bedroom upstairs, which would entail building stairs, plus dormers on the roof. It would cost a minimum of $50,000. That's where she stopped short with her renovation plans. At the end of the day, a second bedroom would never compensate for the house's other deficiencies: middle unit, no front yard, no parking, pests. No matter how much money she spent on the house, at a certain point, it was what it was: a little saltbox in an alley behind a restaurant. She'd never get her money out of that house, so she stopped pouring money into it and sold for a tidy profit.

10. **Sell.** Before you spend a dime on renovations, consider putting your house on the market as is, especially if it's a

seller's market and you have a lot of equity in your home. But do a little remodeling and staging. In the bathroom, keep it simple: Paint the walls, regrout, install a new toilet seat and shower curtain. Replace kitchen cabinet doors only, and maybe put in stainless-steel appliances—but buy them used and refurbished at a fraction of the cost. Sometimes that's all you need to do to make the sale.

CHAPTER 12

Cash in the Cradle

We all know fairy tales don't usually come true. Children aren't deposited at your doorstep by money-savvy storks, just as your debts are paid off and the moving boxes are dropped in the foyer of your first house, for which you put down at least 20 percent. In fact, kids have a way of throwing all your financial plans out the window, because they cost money, period. How much? Somewhere between "more than you can imagine" and "not nearly as much as you think."

A few years ago, *Time* magazine reported that raising a kid to the age of eighteen costs the average family more than $200,000. That's without a postsecondary education. Add that, and you can more than double, maybe even triple, that figure, depending on where that kid goes to school and whether you're going to pay for it. (And remember, that's not a given, in my opinion. You should not put your retirement income in jeopardy in order to finance your child's postsecondary education.)

Mind you, having fewer children means fewer people contributing to the social safety net, so your retirement plans had better be based on the idea of self-sufficiency. You won't have kids to take you to the eye doctor, or someone to check in on you at home. More important, you can't move in with them in your old age if they don't exist. You'll need to hire people to take care of you, so you'd better budget accordingly.

Kids enrich your life, but it's important to understand that they are not free. The financial responsibility they bring with them is immense. These are my children, Savannah and Trevor, when they were young. *(Kevin O'Leary)*

Money Mistake: You're Not Sure You Can Afford Kids

THE FIX: CRUNCH SOME BABY NUMBERS

However lovely it is to have kids, they are financial drains: the shoes, the clothes, food, day care, gasoline, prom dresses, ski trips, lunch money. It doesn't stop for almost two decades. And now, with so many of them moving back home because the economy keeps kicking them to the curb, you have to ask yourself if you can really afford to raise one or two of them for a quarter of a century. As you've read, the financial burden of a grown kid who doesn't contribute to the family is huge. Plus, with half of all marriages ending in divorce, you also have to factor in the cost of single parenting, child support, and raising kids in two homes.

But having kids doesn't have to equal going broke, if you make some adjustments. Your lifestyle is going to change drastically. I'm not just talking about your sleep patterns, but eating out, movies, clothing—the things you absentmindedly spent money on. Those days are over. Every dime will begin to matter. You have to have open discussions about maternity leave, who's going to work, who's going to stay home with the baby. You have to find out what you are eligible for in terms of Child Tax Credits and bonuses. Most good day cares cost about $1,000 a month. How are you going to pay for this? Are you eligible for subsidized day care? Also, life insurance and wills—you'll need both now. When it was just the two of you, you could live on the edge a little. But a baby means you have to become much more careful, and you need a clear financial plan in case anything happens to you or your partner.

Then there are the college funds, catastrophe cash, and other investments to consider. It's not just theory anymore. You *need* to set aside money when you have children. It's never been more important to save and invest for the future. So figure out which things you won't miss—the trips, the $25 yoga classes, dinner out three times a week—and funnel that money into your new funds. And by all means, please rethink your plan to buy a house. Consider that you might be better off renting until you're sure you're finished growing your family, even if quarters are cramped for a couple of years. Incurring more debt when you have a baby is a recipe for financial disaster down the road.

Like I said, my kids are the best things that ever happened to me and my wife, but if you're at all ambivalent about the idea of parenting, and especially if money is a real concern, consider not having kids at all. It might be controversial to say this, but no kids means more money to save, invest, and retire on. Being childless means living a different life, for certain, but it can be equally rewarding, especially if you have the money to enjoy it.

Money Mistake: The Baby Is On the Way

THE FIX: DON'T BLOW YOUR SAVINGS ON CONSUMER CRAP

So you went through with it. You've decided to have a child. Great. You've got a budget and a financial plan for that in place, right? We're often told that the first year of a baby's life is the priciest—the new furniture, the doodads and gadgets you're supposed to buy to get ready for baby. There's an insidious consumer trance that comes over new parents. Successful big-box stores and retailers now have entire corporate wings devoted to selling parents new clothes and designer furniture. Setting up a nursery has become a competitive parental sport, a far cry from the days when a bassinet at the foot of the bed was all you needed besides diapers and a baby bottle. Some estimates put the cost of the baby's first year at $10,000. That's not including the increase in utility bills, from running the dishwasher, washer, and dryer three times more than you used to.

I have a colleague in television, a bright guy who's also pretty financially savvy. He watches the markets. He knows what's what about money. When his partner got pregnant, he did a few things right—chief among them, he and his partner didn't go on a consumer baby binge the moment the pregnancy test came back positive. To all new parents out there: It's a baby. It doesn't need a whole lot of stuff besides love and food. This couple I mentioned spent exactly $100 to prepare for their newborn. They bought some diapers and wipes and bottles. That's it. The baby bassinet, the state-of-the-art car seat, the stroller, the clothing, the blankets—that stuff was all donated by their friends and family whose own children had grown out of it. This not only demonstrates good spending habits; this is good parenting. Being frugal from the get-go instills in a child the difference between need and want. By the way, the stuff passed down to them was good quality. Rather than giving it away, their friends and family might have made a buck on the resale. I'm just saying.

Money Mistake: Your Child Can't Take No for an Answer

THE FIX: STRENGTHEN YOUR NOS OR LEAVE THE KID AT HOME

The baby is doing fine, growing fast, and before you know it, you've got a toddler on your hands. I've stepped around many a toddler arched in full-body tantrum, refusing to stop crying or leave the store until Mom or Dad buys him or her the thing the toddler desperately wants. It's ugly. The parents, traumatized by their child's embarrassing public behavior, tell themselves they'll give in *just this once*. But what they don't realize is that by giving in financially, they animate the dormant spending zombie in their children. The child learns that losing control is a good way to control the parents' spending habits. The parents feel the only way to appease the child is to purchase something to shut the child up. It's a toxic combination—and marketing, advertising, even product placement in big-box stores encourage the continuation of this terrible habit.

My wife used to take a minute before bringing our kids into such volatile environments as toy stores, carefully outlining exactly what was going to happen in that store. She'd tell them they were there to buy a gift for a cousin or for a friend's birthday party, and they weren't buying anything else. So Savannah and Trevor understood what was going to occur before they could even begin bargaining. (By the way, a child in the middle of intense bargaining is a thing to behold. I sometimes wish I could hire toy-motivated children to sell mutual funds.)

I've made a lot of mistakes as a parent, but here's something I will say we did right: My wife and I said no to our children really, really well. Our nos were so solid, they could have been carved into the side of Mount Rushmore. My nos have gotten a little less rigid over the years as my kids have grown into hardworking young adults. But your first no matters. It lays the groundwork for all future financial negotiations with your kids, so it's got to have strength. If you're in a parenting partnership, both of you have to be on the same page. The minute the child senses a crack in the bond, he or she turns ferocious. But saying that you don't have the money to buy something isn't really a great idea, either. It implies that if you did have the money, the kid would be getting a different answer. That's why no means no. Period.

There was a time when kids didn't go to toy stores. They weren't invited to every dinner party, either, and they certainly didn't get to eat in fine restaurants. Going to the mall wasn't a twice-weekly trip. It was saved for special occasions. Times are different now. Before your children participate in the adult consumer culture, they must be taught about money, its value, and who holds the purse strings in the family. And they must know it's not them.

5 Ways to Minimize Baby-Spending Madness

Introducing a child into your life doesn't mean you have to throw financial wisdom out the window. It means you need to be even more frugal now. Here are some tried-and-true tips my mother would agree with.

1. **Clothes.** Kids grow. All your new-baby needs are cotton onesies they can throw up on. They need a ton of those and some blankets. The mini-peacoat, the tiny leather biker jacket? Really? Skip them.

2. **Strollers.** It's sickening how expensive these things are. Growing up, I don't remember a lot of people even owning strollers. Now they're as tricked out as small vehicles, and often as big. Buy a good-quality used one.

3. **Day care.** This is a tricky topic because it involves conversations about who will stay home with the child and who will continue to work. In an era in which it can cost more than $800 a month for full-time day care, these are worthy conversations. Do the math. If it turns out that living on one income will save you thousands of dollars in transportation costs, it might be worth it to forgo day care. Or ask friends or family nearby if they'll help out. Pay them, though. Don't prey on the goodwill of Grandma

when it comes to caring for your kids. That creates bad Money Karma.

4. **Expensive baby toiletries.** If it was good enough for your mother to use on you, it's probably good enough for you to use on your baby. Stick to the simple stuff: baby oil, baby soap, and baby shampoo from the drugstore. Your baby does not need high-end skin care products. (By the way, *you* probably don't, either.)

5. **Fancy toys.** They clutter the house and spoil the kid. Lots of them are toxic hazards. Most kids, when given a choice between a multicolored, germ-infested activity center and a cardboard box filled with a bunch of Tupperware, will choose the Tupperware every time. We used to give my daughter, Savannah, old magazines to rip to shreds when she was a baby. When that bored her, emptying the contents of my wife's purse and filling it back up again would occupy her for a few more hours. (And my wife learned to keep the clutter in her purse to a minimum . . . and never to carry sharp objects or lipstick.)

CHAPTER 13

Avoiding Money Pits

No matter how you cut it, the economy is inextricably linked to the rise and fall of the auto industry. And how we live our lives, where we live and work, and how we get around are all defined by our relationship to the car, whether we own one or not. In other words, cars are here to stay, and increasingly in some parts of the world, such as China and India, you don't have to be part of the middle class to afford them.

But cars also constitute the single biggest money pit many of us own, after our homes. Cars need gas, upkeep, to be stored and parked, cleaned and tuned. Let's look at the average cost of a midpriced sedan such as a 2013 Toyota Camry LE. It'll cost you about $24,000 outright to buy one. But according to the American Automobile Association, to keep it on the road each year, your fixed costs (insurance, license/registration, and depreciation) will be another $8,946.

The most insane aspect of owning a car is that, while it depreciates in value, your output (the money you spend to keep it on the road) only increases. Even for a newer car, like that 2013 Toyota. Then there's the cost of keeping gas in the car, which according to the Bureau of Labor Statistics will set you back another $2,655 per year. That's the country's average fuel cost, but some cities, such as San Francisco, post higher gas prices because of the longer commutes.

So all told, your average car will cost you $11,601 a year to keep on the road. Maybe that doesn't come as a shock to you. That's fine. I'm just asking you to be aware not just of the sticker price of common money pits, but of any and all continuing costs involved with products and services you buy into. Cars are costly and voracious, and some people simply opt to go without. But that's not possible for many people.

Owning a car, however, doesn't mean we can't be financially smarter about them. Do you really need the tinted windows, the fancy rims, the extended warranties, the heated seats, and the sunroof? Probably not. The goal of every good marketer is to make you fall in love with a big purchase so that every single incremental cost associated with that purchase feels vital and necessary. But car extras add up to thousands of dollars. And if you're thinking about resale, the only things people look for in terms of extras are air-conditioning and a decent stereo system. Most people will take low mileage over racing stripes any day. Also, don't accept the sticker price of a vehicle, especially a used one. Shop around, compare prices, and bring lower ones in writing to the dealership. And play hardball. Dealers want to move cars. The first price is never the final price.

Same goes for insurance. Shop around. Fees vary wildly from company to company, and if you have a clean driving history, you should be able to negotiate a better price. And don't go crazy on insurance. If you're driving an older vehicle whose resale value is less of a concern, skip collision coverage. So what if someone dings your car? It's often cheaper for you to pay for that out of pocket than to pay the insurance costs over time. If you are concerned about your car's appearance, then keep collision for a few years, but once it's past the point of a meaningful resale value, drop it.

Your other option is to move downtown. Or, if you live in a suburb, move to a city. Again, you can still keep your car for big grocery runs or dropping the kids off at the arena at dawn. But city dwellers tend to walk everywhere, and after paying $20 a day for parking, you might be inclined to commute to work on foot. Never a bad idea. And buy a home near all the amenities you need. No use being near a grocery store, but far from the nearest dry cleaner or vet. Be strategic. What constitutes an amenity for you might not be necessary for someone else. Whatever you need your car for, buy near those shops and services and watch your savings grow. The cost of renting a downtown loft might be a little higher than that of leasing a house in the suburbs. But factor in the savings on transit costs, gas, bus or commuter train fares, parking, and insurance, and you're probably saving money.

But here's the best cost-saving advice: If you buy, consider buying used. The best reason to buy used vehicles is that the car's depreciation value was someone else's problem. What you're buying is simply a car worth X amount. But before you sign anything, make sure you take the used car to a mechanic you trust or one recommended by a friend.

I mentioned I bought a Porsche, which I call my midlife crisis vehicle. I love it, but it's the biggest waste of money on the planet, up there with my lake house, which requires a fortune in upkeep. I can afford these indulgences and luxuries, but you will never hear me justifying them or calling them investments. I work hard, and I reward myself—within my means. But I curse that car every time a $2,000 flat tire or $5,000 electrical glitch crops up.

Money Mistake: Your Car Is Eating Your Cash

THE FIX: LEASE YOUR VEHICLE OR BUY USED

If you can't go completely car-free, here's something to consider: Leasing a car often makes more sense than buying a car, especially if you're financing the purchase. As you know, I like certainty. I like knowing my monthly nut. Leasing a car doesn't require a huge down payment, and I know that if the transmission blows or the timing belt cracks, I can take it in for repairs, usually for free. And if I lease an outright lemon, it'll be replaced. Leasing costs a certain amount over a certain period of time, and when that time's up, I can swap my car for a new vehicle, or purchase it at its remaining value.

Wait a minute, you say. Isn't it better to be building equity in your vehicle by buying it rather than essentially renting a car by leasing? Only if you can afford to buy it outright, which most people can't. However, if you do think you're going to drive the same vehicle for fifteen years, buying's always the better option, especially if you know you're going to exceed mileage restrictions that come with most leased vehicles. But most people aren't going to do that. And they like to drive a new or newer car every few years.

When you buy, also keep in mind the rapid depreciation most new cars undergo during their first few years, sometimes as high as 20 percent the minute you drive a new car off the lot. If you can't afford a healthy down payment that'll cover some of that early depreciation, you can find yourself in that awful place commonly called an "upside-down" loan, or negative equity situation. That's where you're making car payments on a vehicle that is no longer worth anywhere near its original price. Your balance is $10,000, but if you were to sell the car, you'd be lucky to get $8,000. That's why renters did better than homeowners during the mortgage crisis, when housing values plummeted, yet people were stuck with mortgages they'd negotiated to finance the bloated price of the home. Renters could walk away if a landlord hiked up the rent, but for homeowners it often meant borrowing more money, declaring bankruptcy, or defaulting on their mortgage.

Leasing a car means there is certainty; with financing, there are many variables—too many, especially when it comes to care and maintenance costs. You absorb 100 percent of those costs as the owner.

Money Mistake: You Have a Thing for Bling

THE FIX: DON'T GET DAZZLED, GET EDUCATED

Since the beginning of time, people have been suckers for shiny things, and not just shiny cars. I'm talking about smaller, more sparkly money pits: jewelry, or "bling." Earrings, bracelets, watches, rings, and necklaces have become a part of almost every important ceremony and rite of passage known to humankind. You know who knows that investing in jewelry is a phenomenal waste of money? Rich people. They're often the least ostentatious people I know (not counting the late Elizabeth Taylor or the queen).

Take Barbara Corcoran, a fellow Shark and a woman worth about $40 million. I once commented on a nice pearl necklace she had on, and when she told me the price, I nearly choked. Not because it was so expensive. Quite the opposite. I couldn't believe how *little* it cost. Barbara describes her style as "easy and simple," and she's not the kind of woman who's dazzled by brand names and inlaid diamonds. Barbara and I don't always see eye to eye on things, but when she told me she spent $10 on that necklace in Chinatown, I've never admired her more. Sometimes she wears a different pearl necklace that cost $120, and she's gone on record saying you can't tell the difference. For once I agree with her.

Skip that huge outlay of cash, or put it toward a true investment. Because gold and diamond values rise and fall sharply with the commodities markets. Do your research before investing, and never invest more than 5 percent in any one category—that includes gold. Not to mention, jewelry often gets lost or stolen and is hard to insure. And if you do get insurance, the cost of the premiums can erode the face value of the jewelry. The other problem is that quality is subjective. Appraisers will vary wildly in their assessment of a piece of jewelry's value. Again, do your research and get recommendations from people who know more about this than you.

The thing I hate the most about jewelry is the markups. If you want to go cheap, buy the diamond separate from the setting, and bargain hard for both. Jewelry salespeople are worse than used car dealers. Bring someone experienced to haggle for you. I bought my wife a gem when we got engaged, and she picked out the setting. It wasn't just cheaper, it made the gift more personal, and she had control over the tricky parts, the metal for the band and the fit.

Mostly jewelry breaks my number-one rule when it comes to money and investing: Emotions are often involved. If there is a sentimental value attached to a locket or diamond, you will always be reluctant to part with it. Then you're sitting on a dead investment.

Money Mistake: Your Gym Costs a Fortune

THE FIX: WALK IT OFF

Committing to a healthy lifestyle is crucial at any age, and seniors need to keep active, too, often on tight budgets. When you're thinking about keeping fit, think of your body, but also your pocketbook. By some reports, obesity costs the United States $190 billion in lost productivity and associated health expenditures. But that would assume that people who need the gym are the ones actually joining, and that's not necessarily the case. People who join gyms are generally into fitness, so the gym is more of a social club than the only means of getting some exercise.

And gyms are expensive social clubs, as well as insidious money pits. Most gym memberships require an up-front registration fee of several hundred dollars, and then a monthly payment that's anywhere from $30 to $100 or more, depending on the amenities. So on average, you're paying about $1,000 a year. Again, worth it if those millions of people were committed, the pounds dropped off, and health care costs plummeted. That'd be a good investment.

But for most people, buying a gym membership is like subscribing to a magazine they never read. Every month, they pay money to a company that provides them with something they pretty much throw away, and they continue to pay for the privilege. According to some reports, four out of five gym memberships go unused after the first three months. That's a significant drop-off, and a big waste of money.

You might be surprised to learn that I don't advocate building a home gym of any kind, either. All those gizmos get thrown under the bed after one or two uses. And a treadmill eventually becomes an expensive clothes hanger in most people's bedrooms, yet they're still making payments on it. So don't get lulled into buying that elliptical because you think you'll save on a gym membership. You're spending the same amount, but on a different useless gadget. If you really want to get fit and save some money, start walking everywhere. I can't stress this alternative enough. In fact, if you live within an hour's walk to work, by leaving the car at home a few times a week, you're getting most—if not all—of the exercise you really need. And it's the best kind there is: low impact, outdoors, easy on the joints and the wallet.

Also, many specialty channels on TV and online cater to precisely the kind of exercise you want to do, from aerobics to yoga to Pilates. Not only are there more options than at a gym, but you can exercise when it's convenient for you. Plus you'll save on parking and gas.

These days, gyms are responding to pressure to be more flexible with their payment systems. Some will let you pay as you go, or pay for five-, ten-, or twenty-class packages. To avoid hidden costs or being charged for time you didn't agree to, pay for your membership in cash. That way, the gym doesn't have access to your credit card and won't be able to make automatic renewals.

Gyms cost a lot because they cover a lot of square footage and real estate is expensive. That's why boot camps in parks and informal running clubs are also becoming more popular. There are no monthly fees; it's a pay-as-you-sweat system that costs around $15 to $20 per class. The downside is that classes are usually available only in the summer. So Google around and see what's available in your area. If camaraderie is what you crave with gym memberships, then join a running club. You get the group support that makes it more likely you'll stick to your regimen, without all the costs. If you initiate your own club, then it's free, except for the cost of a good pair of shoes. And don't scrimp here.

I've focused on just a few big money pits into which people can unconsciously sink a lot of their hard-earned income. The problem is that these are rarely one-time purchases. They're continuing financial drains, the cost of which most people never consider when they make the commitment. So before you commit to continuing costs, be aware of what that money might be better put toward, and how much interest it would earn if deployed elsewhere. That's the essence of the truly savvy spender.

4 More Money Pits to Avoid

1. **Vacation properties and lake houses.** First, there's the purchase price, which can be anywhere from $200,000 to millions of dollars, if you want a prime waterfront location in Cape Cod or Lake Tahoe. But upkeep alone could take away a big chunk of your income. Think about it: You are stocking another house with food, furniture, and bedding. Then, you're spending hundreds of dollars a month in gas to drive for several hours every weekend. Not to mention the utilities, taxes, insurance, road maintenance, docking fees, and the care and maintenance of a boat, if necessary. Some estimates say that basic lake-house upkeep takes a minimum of $10,000 a year, not including money set aside for emergencies, such as a new roof or dock. My lake house is one of my single biggest expenses, and while I hate

Our lake house. Sometimes real estate is not an investment, it's
a money pit. Consider renting—it's often a better option.
(Kevin O'Leary)

writing those checks for the boathouse renovations, I love
dangling my feet in the water. But I don't kid myself. It's not
an investment, it's an indulgence.

2. **Swimming pools.** So you won't get a lake house, but you'll
   install an in-ground swimming pool so the kids can hang
   out in the backyard for the summer. Installation can cost
   anywhere from $25,000 to $50,000. That doesn't include
   the new fence with the kidproof lock and the new patio
   furniture. And don't count on the kids to care for and
   maintain the pool. They'll talk the big talk and make all
   sorts of promises, but when it comes down to cleaning and
   vacuuming the pool, it's going to be either you or someone
   you hire. Add the cost of chemicals, filters, and a higher
   electrical bill and you're looking at paying about 10 percent

of the pool's initial costs, per season. That's the estimate a reputable pool company will give you. Installing a $30,000 pool? You're paying $3,000 a season to keep it clean and safe. But the biggest concern is resale value on your house. Always remember that your idea of summer fun is a prospective buyer's idea of a big headache.

3. **Expensive sports.** I'll be forever grateful that neither of my kids was interested in sports like hockey, ice skating, or baseball. Not only am I cheap, but I hate the hours: getting up at the crack of dawn to schlep them to the arena or skating rink . . . no, thanks. If your kid's been bitten by the hockey bug, *Forbes* estimates you'll spend $1,500 to $3,000 in gear alone, and if the team travels, you can tack another $1,000 to $3,000 onto the budget. Does your kid love figure skating? Private coaching and rink time cost between $200 and $300 a month. You'll easily spend over $200 on new skates, and competitions cost hundreds of dollars—not counting hotels and other travel costs. Even baseball bats can run $300 to $400 for the high-end stuff. And of course, your kids will outgrow their equipment and uniforms quickly; that's what kids do. Yes, there are equipment swaps, and a community rec center or the YMCA might offer cheaper options than private teams and clubs. But unless your child is really passionate about these sports or shows signs of being the next Wayne Gretzky or Michelle Kwan, thereby ensuring a return on your investment, sign him or her up for soccer or basketball instead.

4. **Special diet plans.** You've seen the ads. For as little as $25, you can lose twenty-five pounds. But what those ads fail

to mention is that their program costs a little bit of money to join, but a fortune to lose the weight. That's because you're buying *their* food and *their* supplements, which is how those companies make *their* fortune. It's one of the biggest rackets on the planet. People either never lose the weight or rarely keep it off, yet they all too readily sign up for the next new thing to promise that this time it'll work. Depending on how many of the services and products you buy, a popular weight-loss program can cost you between $5,000 and $10,000 a year. Instead, consult your family doctor about a personalized diet plan. It's free, safe, and as effective as anything else.

MIDLIFE MONEY MATTERS & YOUR FINANCIAL LEGACY

My brother, Shane, and my mother, Georgette, on the dock at Lake Geneva in December 2001. Georgette was a shrewd investor; she drilled the never-spend-the-principal mantra into our heads at an early age. She never bought a stock that did not pay a dividend. Today's billion-dollar O'Leary Funds Mutual Funds Company was built on her value-yield philosophy.
(Kevin O'Leary)

CHAPTER 14

Midlife and Money Karma

Here's what I have learned as I head toward my own twilight years: Nobody gets away with anything. If you didn't work like a dog in your twenties, and you blew your money in your thirties and forties, you're going to have to scrimp like crazy in your fifties and keep working well into your sixties. If you stood in line every morning at Starbucks and dropped $5 on those fancy, foamy drinks in your twenties and thirties, you'll be serving the same suckers in your sixties and seventies with that part-time barista job you need to subsidize your meager income. If you took ill-advised risks with your investments, you're going to have to pay for that in your golden years, too.

That's Money Karma in action: reward or punishment, depending on your previous financial actions. Good Money Karma works like this: If you had a good financial plan and instituted it, you probably have enough. Now it's time to start giving back. In their later years, my mother and stepfather nestled into a comfortable retirement in Switzerland, but neither one of them ever stopped working. George never really retired. For fifteen years, he continued to consult for the World Bank and other UN organizations, making less money but gaining a greater sense of purpose because the economic policies he proposed helped people better their lives, especially financially. And as I mentioned, my mother volunteered with women's organizations at the UN. Thirty years ago, she and a handful of friends began to make dolls and scarves sold at a bazaar to raise money for children's causes around the world. It was informal at the start. Mostly, it was an excuse for them to get together and socialize while doing something purposeful. Soon, other embassies started to sell things at the bazaar—maple syrup from the Canadian embassy, handicrafts from Nepal, and perfume from the French embassy. This small group that called itself the United Nations Women's Guild eventually corralled forty embassies in Geneva to participate. Today, this one-day UN bazaar brings in as much as $300,000 in sales, all donated to charity. That money has built sports facilities in Bogotá and treated children with cancer in Egypt. My mother was as proud of that work as anything she'd ever done in her life—Money Karma in its purest form.

But give only if you can afford to give, which means only if you've paid off all your debts. I like to set aside at least 5 percent of my after-tax income, funneling it to a few select charities that mean something to me and my wife, such as foundations that fight disease, or arts and cultural organizations. We call our charitable donations "five in five." We select five charities or causes for five years and support those, rather than spreading our focus too widely. After five years pass, we assess and choose five more. The method doesn't matter; the point is that good Money Karma goes beyond any tax break you'll receive. There are health benefits to giving. Countless academic studies have come to the same conclusion: Altruistic people live longer, healthier, and happier lives. Therefore, they're less of a financial burden on their families and on society. You give, you get.

But Money Karma works not only with giving, it works with spending. And midlife is not the time to be messing with that karma.

Money Mistake: The Nest Felt Empty, You Bought a Dog

THE FIX: BUDGET FOR BOWSER BEFORE YOU BUY

The kids are out of the house, you've been aggressively paying down your mortgage, you're almost debt-free, and you're feeling your Money Karma aligning in the best possible way. Then you go out and get yourself a dog, reversing all that good karma. It's baffling to me that getting a dog has become synonymous with winding down into midlife and eventually retirement. For all it costs to keep a pet alive, happy, and healthy, we should be feeding it a steady diet of shredded cash. Don't even get me started on what it costs to keep that animal clothed. Yes, clothed. I wouldn't call myself an animal lover, but I do have great respect for animals. So I feel their pain when I see them dolled up in dresses and hats, being paraded around wearing an umbrella strapped to a harness. Idiotic.

We see them every year on *Shark Tank*—entrepreneurs with the latest in doggy gadgets and fashions, including neoprene booties and plaid raincoats, doggie diapers and cat boxes that fit on windowsills, pendants that contain your pets' cremains . . . and the list goes on. And every year, I go from being amused at the bulldog on the skateboard to being incensed at the poodle in the stroller. Why? Because there are people out there who will buy these completely asinine gadgets, people who might even carry a lot of debt, who will put shoes on their dogs even if it means spending the last dollar in their pocket. That said, I have admittedly gone into bidding wars for some of the more insidious animal ideas that I know will make big bucks.

Someone once said, "A pet is a short story with a sad ending." I say, "A pet is an *expensive* story, with an *expensive* ending." I'm going to give it to you bluntly: A pet is a phenomenal waste of money. Few people actually consider the cost of a pet *before* getting one. They factor in the fun and affection, but they forget about the food, the license, the leash, the toys, the treats, the poop bags, the dog-walking services, and the vet.

According to the American Society for the Prevention of Cruelty to Animals, which posts a very detailed outline of pet costs on its website, a medium-sized mutt will cost $1,580, including spaying, in its first year. After that, you're looking at forking over at least $695 a year in vet, food, treats, and doggie day-care costs. As for cats, their start-up costs are estimated at $365, and then you pay $670 a year in kitty upkeep. Consider that cats and dogs live longer than ever before—upward of fifteen years in some cases. That means you should budget more than $12,000 in a lifetime for the privilege of pet ownership. In fact, there are some surveys that put the lifetime cost of a fifteen-year-old dog way over the $30,000 range. That's assuming no surprise vet visits for broken doggie bones, dental work, swallowed socks, or hip dysplasia, let alone continuing costs to treat diabetes or thyroid conditions. In fact, consider vet insurance if you're not budgeting for the doggie emergency room.

If these costs don't deter you and you still want to make room for Fido or Fluffy, then do your research and stick to a manageable breed, one that isn't prone to pricey health issues. For my money, mutts and mixed-breed animals are always the healthier, heartier choice. And stay away from pet stores and breeders.

Adopt your animal from a reputable shelter where it is sure to be spayed or neutered and arrive with all its shots. Or better yet, volunteer as a dog walker at your local Humane Society. Or foster an animal—you'd be doing a community service, but the best part? Food and medicine are free to you. All you need to do is take care of the animal until it's adopted, because you're not going to fall in love with it and completely defeat the purpose of this exercise. Right? Plus, you'll get some valuable (and free) dog-walking training, which you can monetize to make some extra money on the side. This is a great way for cash-strapped retirees to pick up some extra cash and get a little exercise to boot.

If all else fails, get a fish. They're easy to feed. Easy to dispose of when they die. No vet bills. In fact, get two.

Money Mistake: The War on Aging Is Expensive

THE FIX: CHOOSE YOUR WALLET OVER YOUR FACE

No generation has wanted to stay forever young more than the baby boomers. Maybe because unlike young people today, we lived in flush times. When we cast our eyes backward, the times were indeed better. At least economically speaking. And just when we finally have pantloads of cash, we look in the mirror and realize we're middle-aged.

You've probably heard me say this on TV: Antiaging services have the best profit margins on the planet, and they're the worst wastes of money ever. Women are the biggest market out there for age-defying "solutions." Did you know that the only companies that don't suffer much during hard economic times are those in the beauty industry? People losing everything want to look good. That's why I like to invest in cosmetics companies.

But in the interest of saving you money, I'm going to state a few things unequivocally: Botox and fillers probably won't make you look younger, just different, and in many cases, they actually make you look worse—that's karma in action. And that's also just my opinion.

The point is, beyond the aesthetics of these procedures, once you go down the Botox and filler route, you've become just another revenue stream for a multibillion-dollar cosmetics industry. These companies will do everything in their power to make you continually chase results that will remain elusive. And in many cases, you have to keep injecting hundreds of dollars of chemicals into your face every few months until you die, which is why I say investing trumps injecting. They're lifetime financial commitments, results not guaranteed. Botox costs on average about $400 per treatment, and it's recommended you get injected three times a year, at a cost of $1,200. And if you start in your forties and stop in your sixties, say, you're blowing up to $24,000 on procedures that haven't actually added much value to your life.

So save a dime and stop buying beauty magazines. They're brainwashing you into thinking that beauty is only about youth and thinness. According to online consumer guides and many honest experts, the cream you buy at the local pharmacy is often as effective as the high-end product. In other words, repair your finances, not your face. You're going to get old anyway, so why waste money avoiding the inevitable? In my TV work, I have yet to see a face filled with chemicals that looks great. Instead, be graceful about getting old, because when it comes to feeling youthful, vital, and energized, no amount of Botox beats money in the bank.

Measure Your Midlife Money Karma

By the time you're inching toward middle age, money should be coming back to you as a reward for good decisions. But sometimes one bad financial decision can reverse your fortune *overnight*. Great investments are poured into a bad business idea. A family loan wipes out your savings. Adult children chip away at your retirement income. A midlife crisis is solved with a red Ferrari. Take this test to see in what direction your Money Karma is flowing.

1. **The kids are finally out of the house (which is almost fully paid for), and you and your partner want to begin enjoying life. The first thing you do is:**
   a) take stock of your money by recording another 90-Day Number, possibly making adjustments to your retirement plans, depending on where you are financially.
   b) consider putting the house on the market. Might be time to liquidate and downsize.
   c) book an around-the-world cruise. You deserve it. You've just put two kids through college and the house is almost paid for. Time to splurge.

If you answered A, it's a surefire way to keep your Money Karma flowing in a positive direction. I'm not a fan of making rash financial decisions before understanding all the numbers in play. If you've put your kids through college, bought a lake house, or made any other big midlife commitment, you must reevaluate your finances. One big shift will have a huge impact on when you can retire and on how much. So doing another 90-Day Number exercise is a great way to watch your expenditures.

Scenario B might not be a bad idea, but if you're still making mortgage payments and the end is near, perhaps wait until you're mortgage-free for a little while, saving and investing what were your mortgage payments into a conservative retirement vehicle, such as bonds. And please consult a good real estate agent, and a financial advisor if you plan to liquidate and rent. You want to minimize your tax impact and maximize your equity to keep that karma in the black and not the red.

And if you're all for C, tread the next few years carefully. I can't tell you how many times I've heard the stories of midlife spending sprees that tap out a family's savings. Now's not the time to rip through a $25,000 dream vacation. Illness, accidents, and any number of emergencies can befall us in middle age. So maintain that good Money Karma and keep a lid on big purchases, at least until you get your full financial picture.

2. **Your parents are in financial trouble. Your dad made a late-in-life investment in an orchard that had a few bad seasons, and your mom is sick and needs expensive treatment. They've come to you for help. You have the money, but it would jeopardize your own retirement plans. You offer to:**

   a) help comb through their finances to unearth money they probably didn't know they had, and find treatment alternatives that your parents might better afford. In other words, you don't panic. You help them help themselves, but you don't give them money you can't afford to give.

   b) rally the whole family behind them, including siblings and cousins, so you're not the only one carrying the financial burden. And you make it a loan.

c) write them a check. They're your parents, after all, and
they did everything for you when you were growing up.

This is one of the toughest financial conundrums there is, which is why I bring it up a lot in this book. I am trying to hammer home the idea that your money is there to save your life, not other people's lives. So answering A is a way to keep Money Karma moving in the right direction, while still being of some help to your parents. Sometimes, bad financial situations are really just a lack of clarity and a misunderstanding of options. Offering to be the clear set of eyes is a great way to be of service without getting mired in their problems. Maybe they can sell off some assets? Maybe they qualify for tax deductions generated by the business loss? Maybe your mother hasn't explored all her medical options?

As for B, I think it's a good option, with a few caveats. You never want to be the one who pulls other people into a financial morass no one can get out of. So make sure your parents initiate that discussion with others themselves. But sharing the burden among family does lessen the load for everyone. Ultimately, it's everyone's choice whether to help, but this plan also encourages transparency, which is one of the best ways to straighten out financially and remove the shame from bad money management decisions.

And if you chose C, then I worry for your Money Karma. And your money is worried, too. It knows it's vulnerable from here on in to any and all requests to be depleted, and you had better have a good backup plan yourself, because midlife loans of this caliber *will* wipe out your savings. If you have the extra money, fine, write the check. But as I mentioned before, best not to expect to see that money again.

3. Two of your closest friends have started a small catering business in their midfifties. It's doing pretty well; you even work a function here and there for extra money. But with another $50,000 investment, they say they could have their own kitchen and really expand the business. They've approached you to become a partner. You decide to:

   a) take a pass, but you'll hire them for your retirement party. It's just too much money for you to part with this late in the game. And you're not sure you want to be an entrepreneur after years on a salary. Besides, for every Martha Stewart (who didn't hit big until her forties), there are hundreds, if not thousands, of failed caterers who couldn't differentiate enough to break through.

   b) take it under consideration, but offer a smaller financial commitment of $15,000, increasing your investment as the returns come in. After all, change is good, and you trust these friends to really make a go of it.

   c) take a chance on being part of a new venture. You always fancied yourself an entrepreneur, and what better time to start than right now?

You know I love entrepreneurs. But if there is any doubt in your mind that the entrepreneurial life is for you, A is a wise karmic choice. Also, the big red flag for me is friends getting into business with friends. There is too much room for error, and for emotions to get in the way of business. Add money to the mix, in the form of a hefty investment, and you have a recipe for regret.

Option B isn't terrible, though. If you can invest in tiers, and only if you can afford it, being a silent partner in a growing business might be a way to diversify your investment portfolio. Still, proceed not only with caution, but with experts combing through their books. A proper due-diligence process is in order, no matter how reassuring your friends are. In fact, the more re-assuring they are, the harder the accountants should be breathing down their necks. At any sign of financial dilemma, back out.

And if you picked C again, invest only if you have the money to completely lose. This is a gamble, period. And it's one you can afford to make only if it has little financial impact on your retire-ment plans or your family's future financial stability.

CHAPTER 15

Divorce, Remarriage, and Gold Diggers

When a marriage dissolves in the first few years and no children are involved, there's ample opportunity to recover financially and move on. But midlife divorce constitutes the single biggest erosion of wealth imaginable. Since divorce is a reality for so many people, it's never been a more crucial time to protect your money and proceed with caution. After all, according to some studies, many divorced women experience up to a 25 percent drop in their standard of living (not so shockingly, men experience a 10 percent increase). It's unfair, especially because women are often the primary caregivers of children. That is why, for women, it's never been more crucial to keep your money separate during the marriage. Ladies (and men, too): Make your Secret 10 a chief component of a happy partnership.

If you are thinking of marrying for a second time, you should proceed with even more caution. According to Rutgers University's National Marriage Project, divorce rates for second marriages can be as high as 60 percent. And almost 75 percent of third marriages fail. I think these abysmal marriage stats mirror those for entrepreneurs who serially fail at business after business. Some people aren't cut out to be entrepreneurial, just as some people are not cut out for marriage. And in observing my own social circle, I've noticed that second marriages and even third ones are usually also marked by a rather wide age gap, sometimes as high as fifteen or twenty years. And I'm telling you, those couples rarely make it. Usually, we're talking about an older man/younger woman dynamic, and here's the chief complaint: After the initial excitement wears off, they're generally left with very little in common and even less to talk about. That's just my rudimentary observation.

So if you're going into the second marriage thinking that you needed only to be married to a different person to be happy, think again. And if you had money problems in the first marriage, count on a repeat in the second and third, when you'll probably have even less money to fight over. Blended families are also an expensive proposition. Child support costs are often associated with the first and subsequent marriages, and they follow you down the aisle.

Here's another interesting fact: Late-in-life divorce, or "gray divorce," is on the rise, with many of those proceedings initiated by women who'd rather spend their twilight years alone than in a dead marriage. *But that has created yet another drop in wealth.* In a recent AARP study, 26 percent of couples who got divorced between the ages of forty and seventy-nine reported financial problems. That means late-in-life poverty is a possibility, despite years of disciplined savings and investments.

I talk a lot about separating money and emotions. But I know few people who've successfully pulled that off during divorce proceedings. In fact, divorce is often where emotions reach their crescendo. It's ugly, ugly business. But it's big, big business—$28 billion a year, to be exact. Figures vary across the country, but estimates on the average cost of a divorce range from $15,000 to $30,000. Between court and lawyer's fees and custody and support negotiations, many couples pay closer to $100,000. But the only number you really have to remember is this: The average divorce lawyer charges $200 to $300 *an hour.* Lawyers in certain parts of the United States command closer to $1,000 an hour. Every battle, every dispute, and every disagreement is money in a lawyer's pocket. The greater the conflict, the greater the cost.

The best way to minimize cost is to seek as much parity as possible *before lawyers get involved.* Counseling and mediation are infinitely cheaper. Or you could end up like Janice and Ian, a couple who split after the birth of their second son, after a decade of marriage.

You'd never know it now, but one look at their wedding photo would show you that Ian and Janice were once madly in love. Even their friends would admit they'd have bet money this couple would defy the odds and last a lifetime. But several years into the relationship, Janice began an affair with a colleague while on a business trip. She didn't expect it to last, so she kept it from her husband, thinking it would run its course and fade away. Through a trail of hotel and restaurant receipts (it always comes back to money), Ian discovered the deceit. Rage and jealousy sent him straight to a lawyer rather than seeking counseling or mediation. He immediately fought for full custody of the two boys and the family home. What could have been prevented through counseling or lessened through mediation turned into a full-blown divorce case that dragged its way through court for two years. In the end, a three-month dalliance and a measure of deceit cost the couple $126,000, their entire net worth. Here's the kicker: This couple got back together a few years later. You could call that a happy ending to a sad story, or just a very expensive chapter.

Money Mistake: Divorce Is Killing Your Bottom Line

THE FIX: DON'T LET YOUR MONEY BE THE THIRD CASUALTY IN THE SPLIT

You tried. You really tried. But in the end, divorce remains the last option available to you after a few months of counseling and a cooling-off period during which you lived separate lives in different places. At the end of the day, you still feel divorce is the best way forward, even if your partner doesn't quite agree. This is a common scenario: One wants out of the marriage a little or a lot more than the other. It's not uncontested, it won't necessarily be fully amicable, and yet both partners want to avoid the hell and high cost of going to court.

How do you proceed?

With caution, respect, and whatever amount of love you can still conjure from the early days you were together. It's hard to believe, but the person you're pulling away from was once the love of your life, and if you can exercise a bit of compassion, it'll go a long way toward reducing the most painful costs, especially if you're the one pulling away.

But take it in steps. First, research divorce laws in your state. In North Carolina, for instance, you and your spouse must have lived separate and apart for at least one year before you can divorce. Then, decide with your soon-to-be ex whether mediation can best divide assets and work out custody issues. Do your own photocopying and record-keeping—anything to save money. Put everything in writing, and organize all your assets, income, pensions, debt, investments, and expenses.

When it comes to child support, there are firm tables and guidelines, but these are modifiable. Be generous here. As for property and the marital home, even if you paid for the whole thing, it's usually divided equally. Often, it makes sense for the children to remain with the custodial parent. Some couples even rent separate places where they each live when the children aren't in their primary care. But any money in the children's accounts, such as a trust or any college funds you've set aside, is their money and should remain so.

Seek expert financial guidance to divide any and all assets you've accumulated through investments, property, retirement vehicles, or joint businesses. Don't attempt to do this yourself. Property settlements are final and can't be renegotiated. And don't forget to rewrite and refile a will.

As for working with a lawyer, get a referral from someone you trust, but I suggest you find someone who has a "collaborative practice." This is a relatively new option wherein the lawyer works collaboratively with your soon-to-be ex's lawyer, instead of as an adversary. The goal of a collaborative divorce is to avoid court at all costs, regardless of how acrimonious things might get.

And by all means seek counseling and stay in counseling during the proceedings. It's a good investment that'll go a long way toward reducing the costs of divorce, even years after it's made final. The well-being of any children should always come first.

Money Mistake: You're Dating a Gold Digger

THE FIX: GET A PRENUP

Whether you've weathered an awful divorce or never managed to walk down the aisle to begin with, one of the biggest threats to midlife wealth is people who are after your money: namely, gold diggers. And they're not just for the wealthy to worry about. Anytime there is financial disparity of any kind between a couple, caution must be exercised. If you have a healthy pension, you'd be wise to date someone equally flush in the twilight years.

Then there is the obvious gold digger, the one purely trading youth and beauty for a bit of financial security and bling. I've met a few gold diggers in my travels, both female and male. Some of them are perfectly nice people, but they have a single goal in mind: to meet and marry someone rich. Note: There's a big difference between someone who's concerned about his or her financial health and a gold digger who's interested only in your financial wealth. But the only surefire way to "out" a gold digger is to slap a prenuptial agreement down in front of him or her.

Case in point: I ran into an old acquaintance of mine in New York when my wife and I were attending a party a while ago. My acquaintance is a handsome guy in his midfifties who made his fortune in software, just like I did. Ten years ago, he left his wife and remarried, a union that lasted less than two years and led to a split that cost him hundreds of thousands of dollars. After vowing never to marry again, he then began dating only young, beautiful women who stayed with him as long as the money flowed. These women (classic gold diggers) scrutinized the society pages the way I scrutinize stock prices.

At the party, this acquaintance introduced my wife and me to his latest companion, a bored, leggy redhead decades his junior. After some small talk, the acquaintance and I made plans to catch up over dinner when I was back in New York. A few weeks later, settling into our booth at a swanky steakhouse, I asked about the redhead.

He shrugged. "She's gone," he said. "Engaged to some guy in England."

"Already?" I said, shocked.

He explained that less than a week after we had met her, she was introduced to a British movie mogul. After a few dates, she up and moved to London the minute the mogul committed.

My friend was distressed. He said, "I asked her, 'What does this guy have that I don't?' She said, 'A hundred million dollars.' Then I said, 'What's he giving you that I didn't?' She said, 'A bigger allowance.'"

I burst out laughing at his candor, and hers! At least she wasn't trying to throw love into the equation. This was all about money for her, and getting more of it while she still could. Call her any name you want, but she wasn't stupid.

This phenomenon is everywhere: from the Boston suburbs to the clubs of L.A. We live in a society that places a big premium on youth and beauty, and a lot of young people know this. I don't mean to insult the millions of young people out there who'd never choose their date according to wallet size.

"Some gold diggers actually do have hearts of gold." These are the words of Gerald Sadvari, one of the top divorce lawyers in the land. Part of his job is putting a tricky price tag on the value of a woman (or man) between the ages of twenty-four and thirty-eight, the average age of the so-called gold digger. He describes the classic gold-digger dynamic like this: old guy, young woman. The old guy's marrying her only to bask in the corona of her youth and beauty, both of which are beginning to elude him. And she's hoping to get pampered and spoiled while she's young and pretty. Sex figures in, no doubt, but that's none of my business. She probably suffers from the disease of "more." Her rich compatriot, however, suffers from the disease of "not enough"—not enough glory, not enough recognition, not enough reassurance that he's top dog in whatever field he works in. So he needs a symbol in the form of a human being to show the world—and other men—that he's a winner. No matter what the dynamic, if there's an ironclad prenup, the richer party will usually survive if it comes down to divorce. The gold digger will survive only if he or she has a good prenup, and only until the next sucker comes along.

Part of Sadvari's job is to put a number on the gold digger's value at the end of that relationship. The younger they are, the higher the price. And it makes sense. In the older man/younger woman dynamic, her best years will be spent "off the market," so to speak.

A number of elements factor into Sadvari's equation—for instance, what she does for a living and whether marrying the man means she'll have to give that up, and her lifestyle expectations for herself and any children she may bring into the marriage. It's a fascinating idea, placing a money value on youth and fertility, but that's the cold hard truth. Lots of women walk away when they realize that, in the event of divorce, the marriage won't yield them any gains. But some persevere.

At his office, Sadvari keeps a box of Kleenex in the cabinet behind him. Tears tend to flow when people are talking about money, motives, and marriage. He told me about a young client who took one look at a prenuptial agreement, one that would leave her with next to nothing if she and her partner split. That's when the waterworks began. Drying her eyes, she asked for advice.

"I didn't want to interfere, but I made it pretty clear that the guy in the equation was overreaching," he said. "Overreaching" is a legal way of saying he built a legal fortress around his fortune, one that would be impenetrable even to a clever judge. This, Sadvari suggested, indicated that the relationship she was in might not be a great one on which to bet her youth.

"This woman, however, went ahead with the marriage, knowing full well she was getting nothing at the end." Twenty-five years later, that couple is still together, Sadvari said. It was a love match. She became a force on the philanthropy front, and he is a happy and supportive husband. The prenup was a gamble that worked out for both parties.

But for every happy ending, Sadvari has also seen how massive wealth can be eroded in just one generation by a succession of marriages that cost a small fortune in divorces. One of his clients is on his fourth marriage. He is more broke than he's ever been, but he didn't have the heart to institute fierce prenups.

"What can I say? The guy's a romantic," Sadvari laments.

I want to be clear: Pushing for greater parity in a prenup because you have to give up a job or leave the country or take care of children in this new partnership isn't gold-digging. This is smart premarital negotiating. But if you're concerned only about your cut in case the marriage ends, you should both know what you're getting into.

Even a true gold digger deserves a little financial advice. Here's mine: I suggest that you learn a skill as part of your exit strategy—and you know you have one, probably many. Get your real estate license or some chef training, because those are the kinds of jobs that pay well and require really good contacts, which you'll have. Your backup plan should go beyond getting a cut of someone's wealth, especially if you haven't contributed anything to building it. It should include how you're going to build your own wealth if, or when, things fall apart.

How to Spot a Gold Digger

Not every beautiful young man or woman you meet is out for your money. But I advise you to padlock your wallet or call a lawyer if you are dating people with these characteristics:

- They seem to live beyond their means.
- They have no discernible employment or goals in life beyond being available to you.
- They bring up money way too soon.
- They expect you to pay for everything.
- They wear expensive clothes and jewelry they can't seem to afford.
- They constantly hint at things they'd like you to purchase or pay for.
- They're willing to date someone a lot older and a lot uglier than they are.
- They're cagey about discussing their future or their past, especially other wealthy people they have dated.
- They're less interested in you if you stanch the flow of funds or free stuff.
- They won't sign a prenup.

I'll tell you one thing: No matter your opinion of gold diggers, we can all learn something from them—the importance of talking about money in relationships. How can one not have a grudging respect for that?

CHAPTER 16

Debt, Divesting, and Downsizing

Broke and in your fifties or even sixties? Look at the bright side: At least gold diggers aren't after your money. If you're cash-strapped, yet still married to that gorgeous blonde who's much younger than you, then at least you've found true love. So be grateful. Then get to work. There's no use berating yourself, or obsessing over how you came to be broke or in debt well past middle age. Put it behind you and make a new plan. First item on your list: Get rid of any and all remaining debt. That is your first and only priority.

According to a recent AARP study, two-thirds of families with a head of household age sixty-five to seventy-four had debt. Of those, more than half owed at least $40,000. American senior citizens are estimated to be the fastest-growing age group to spiral into bankruptcy. It's a generational time bomb. Debt in your later years exacerbates existing health challenges and creates new ones, when you're at your most vulnerable. But here's the good news: It's entirely preventable and entirely curable, but only you can take the proper measures. If the only thing you do right by the time you get to sixty is to retire your debt, all is not lost. There are a few ways to tackle debt so that you can retire with a lot less stress, even if you don't have a lot of money.

For the longest time, a lot of Americans thought that by setting aside a few hundred dollars a month they'd retire as multimillionaires. I blame personal-finance books for that. Many such books show compound interest charts generating 10 percent returns. That's simply not realistic. I know of no financial institution that has delivered steady 10 percent returns over the last ten or twenty years. So the idea of retiring on a fortune by setting aside a little has remained an elusive dream for most people.

So how much do you really need? And when should you panic? First of all, you need less than you'd imagine, and panicking helps nothing. The best antidote to panic is realism. If you hit the age of sixty-five in good health, life is just going to be a lot cheaper to live. If you're realistic.

Let's use a common ratio bandied about—65 percent—which is the percentage of your current gross income that many experts say you'll need to live on when you're old. So if your household makes $100,000 a year today, you'll need $65,000 during year one of your retirement for both you and your spouse. That's including what you'll get from Social Security. Since an average couple will take home $24,500 a year in Social Security, you'll need to top off your income by $40,500 every year. If there are two of you, that's more than $20,000 each, which a million-dollar nest egg generating a 4 percent return can achieve.

But if you have no overhead, no mortgage, no debt, and no dependents, ask yourself what you are going to spend that $65,000 a year on. This assumes that you will want to maintain roughly the same standard of living that you enjoyed when you worked a stressful life, working forty hours a week away from home. Of course, you ate out a lot, bought hardcover books to read on the subway, and got a brand-new coat every winter. But in retirement, you won't need to finance your lifestyle in the same way. There will be no commuting, fewer lunches out, and lower dry-cleaning bills.

You need a million dollars to retire if you have great expectations. If you can achieve that ideal, great—the world will be your oyster. But you can have a fruitful, stable retirement on a lot less, if you adjust your expectations. If you don't think you can go days without spending money on useless crap like magazines, gum, or coffee, then you're going to be in trouble a few years into retirement. If you're healthy and happy, being old is cheap. Walking, working part-time, and living a life of purpose and meaning don't require a lot of money, just planning and discipline. So yes, spend those last few working years socking away as much money as you can, but also use those years to practice living on a lot less, lowering your expectations, and cultivating disciplined spending habits.

Money Mistake: You're Carrying Debt into Retirement

THE FIX: RETIRE DEBT BEFORE YOU RETIRE

If you're heading toward retirement with debt, now's the time to budget like you've never budgeted before. I mean it. You need a black-and-white plan, and you might even need help. Start by following my 90-Day Number plan at the beginning of this book. After you've learned about your personal spending habits and needs, get an advisor, and if you can't afford that, consult a friend who's done everything right—and do what that friend did.

Don't retire until you can afford it. Throw out your plan for freedom at fifty-five or even sixty-five. If you have debt, you need your job, so you have to do everything in your power to keep it. Get a part-time job, too, while you're at it and while you're still spry enough to handle it. I'm not talking about heavy labor. Work the cash register at your local garden center, tutor local kids, or serve coffee. And if you're providing the gift of child care for your beloved grandchildren, you deserve to be getting paid for that.

Refinance your mortgage. If you have been paying off a twenty-five-year mortgage, making $1,000 monthly payments at 4 percent, consider shortening it to fifteen and pay higher rates and monthly payments. Do that while you're working, while you're at your full earning potential. You can also consider a reverse mortgage. I'm not a big fan—there are a lot of fees and hidden costs—but it frees up some equity to tackle that debt. But you'd probably be better off selling the house, paying off the debt, and renting elsewhere.

Also, don't remarry. That said, if you do plan to couple up and live together, make sure, along with a division of money and belongings, to include long-term care plans in your cohabitation agreement. If there are adult children in the mix, also make sure there's an up-to-date will that outlines what your partner should do or will inherit in the event of critical illness, injury, or death.

Get tech-savvy. This is not the time to be a Luddite. You want to know how to Skype your grandchildren, which will save you a fortune on long-distance bills. If you can afford to monetize a hobby, do it. You now have something that was once in short supply: time.

But what about the reader who's well past those prime earning decades and slouching toward retirement trailing a lot of debt and financial regret? When you're sixty years old, broke, and contemplating a sparse retirement, you start thinking about all the stupid crap you bought when you were younger. You have to stop that cycle of regret. It leads to a hopelessness that can only trigger inaction and depression. That money's gone and buried.

I'm a realist. I'm not going to tell you the next decades are going to be easy. It's time to throw out all those expectations you had about how life was going to be in your twilight years. It's time to start planning for something completely different. Here are some cold hard numbers: The average annual income from Social Security is barely over $15,000. As we've seen, that goes up to $25,000 for couples, and if you're a veteran you might qualify for additional government benefits. But that's it, folks. That's poverty-level retirement, no doubt, so you have to be savvy. And very strategic.

But if you're five to seven years away from retirement, you still have a few options to top off that income. You can see how even $5,000 a year more will make all the difference in your quality of life. And if you live another fifteen years after retirement, you're really looking at saving only $75,000 to get to that. You can do that in five to seven years. But you have to be ruthless.

If you're single or widowed, consider getting a roommate or a student boarder. Pooling resources is the smartest thing you can do right now. Radically cut down on all your expenses. Lose the car. Lose the cable. Maybe even lose the cat. You're in an emergency situation. You have to look at every expenditure with a critical eye and make tough decisions about cash flow. If you're fit, stay on that bike and walk everywhere. This will keep you healthy and, more crucially, will lift your mood. Consider

downsizing a little sooner. Pick a place to rent that's close to every amenity you'll need, including a bus stop, a hospital, a grocery store, and a pharmacy. And if you can be closer to family, all the better. You're going to need their help, and they may need yours. But don't skimp on insurance or extra health care benefits, such as dental and a prescription drug plan. This is the decade when health surprises aren't really surprises. Finally, cut off your kids or any other dependents. Anything that isn't being used to support you now is being set aside for your retirement. There is no other money for grown children, no matter how much they beg and plead.

Five to seven years before retirement is the time to practice living frugally. Get used to deprivation before you're deprived. You're trying on what it feels like to live within your new means. And take advantage of everything free coming your way. Some discounts on public transit and event tickets start at sixty, so sign up for everything you're eligible for. Shop on senior-discount days.

More important, start making new friends. It's never too late. You still need a social life and a connection to people your own age. Life's not over. This is just a new phase.

Money Mistake: You're Not Sure When or How to Downsize Your Home

THE FIX: SELL WHEN COSTS OUTWEIGH BENEFITS

Even while they're inching toward retirement, many people sit on their real estate, because they've become emotionally attached to the family home. They remember it as a place where they've raised their kids and they see it as the home their grandchildren will visit. But that home is also a major money pit. It still requires constant upkeep if you want to get your value out of it when you sell, and you're paying increasingly higher taxes on the property. It's also very likely much larger than you actually need. Plus, you still have to insure it. So even if you're mortgage-free, you're certainly not expense-free. Worse, that home is a tempting landing pad for your adult kids, who will always see that bedroom as their bedroom, even if it's been your sewing room for decades.

Sell your home. And don't just move to a smaller house that'll still require a constant outpouring of cash. You're getting older. You can't climb ladders to clean the eaves, and you can't shovel snow forever. And you'll still be paying taxes that'll only go up. Your goal is to reduce consumption and become more self-sufficient, not less. So get an apartment or a condo—something you buy outright, so that your only output is the monthly fee. Or you might consider something you can rent for a long time. Here are some things to consider before selling the family home.

Long before you sell, figure out exactly where you'll live and what you can afford. It's nice to buy near the kids, but do so only if you can afford to live there. Otherwise, the onus is on them to visit you. If you're healthy and like traveling, you might consider another country, such as Costa Rica or Mexico, where your money will stretch further and your kids might not mind visiting.

If you have debt, sell as much stuff as you can before you downsize. Your antique hutch that's worth a fortune, your silver collection, even if it holds sentimental value. Liquidate everything you can. Now's not the time to cry over that grandfather clock. It's time to be pragmatic.

If selling the home will generate a windfall, consider this plan. We have friends who sold their big family home and made a fortune. Some of the proceeds were meant to go to the kids as part of their inheritance. But instead of giving them the cash, the couple bought themselves a nice one-bedroom condo and a couple of studio apartments in the same building for their grown children. Now they're all still living under the same roof, the kids can visit often, but they have their own place to go to, to pay for, and to keep up. I like this plan. You don't have to buy your kids a place outright—a down payment is generous enough—but it's a smart way to liquidate a big asset and pass on a bit of wealth, if that's what you're intending to do anyway.

Invest money from the liquidation wisely and conservatively. Now's not the time to play the markets and take big risks with your portfolio. I strongly advise you to hire a financial advisor, either fee-based or someone who will manage your money for 1 percent (or even less) a year. And skip annuities. They're also loaded with hidden fees. What's crucial is diversification. You never want to invest your final nest egg into any one stock or sector. I repeat: My golden rules of investing are that you put no more than 5 percent in any one stock or bond (always dividend-paying securities) and no more than 20 percent in any one sector. I see this all the time: a fifty-seven-year-old who sells the house and dumps 85 percent of those returns into the stock of a company on the edge of failure. It's a tragedy. The older you get, the more security you need. Remember my rule of thumb about age-based investing: Keep the percentage of bonds you own matching your age. That will stabilize your portfolio and give you a better sense of exactly how much money you have to live on for the rest of your life. Predictability is your friend.

People are not only living longer than their ancestors, they're living healthier lives, too. And yet our workforce is still operating under the old model where people stopped working at sixty-five and lived only another five or ten years. People are living well into their eighties now. And they can easily continue to be vital members of the workforce at least into their seventies. So don't hit the panic button at sixty if you don't have enough saved. You simply have to keep working.

Money Mistake: You Want to Leave Something to Your Kids

THE FIX: DON'T DIVEST UNTIL YOUR LONG-TERM CARE IS COVERED

Nothing creates mushier thinking around money than telling your kids there's a big inheritance waiting for them when you die. Knowing they'll inherit your nest egg encourages dependence and discourages them from building their own. That puts them at a huge competitive disadvantage. It's folly to give them the impression that they don't have to plan for their own retirement because your money is going to come to their rescue. My advice? No inheritances, not a dime, until:

- You're completely covered financially for the rest of your own long life.
- You've accounted for your own emergencies, big and small.
- You've paid off all your debts.
- You've paid for your funeral.
- You've accounted for well-deserved fun and freedom.

We all want to help our kids. We're programmed that way. But you'll be helping them more by taking care of yourself first. Here's the chief reason why I'm against willing money to your kids: If your retirement plans don't include having someone to look after you if you become too old or too sick to do it yourself, you don't have enough money to give to your kids. And please don't assume your children will be willing to take on the task of looking after you when you're unwell, let alone have you move in with them. They may be in no position to do that, and you don't want to place that burden on them any more than they want to take it on.

I don't mean to be bleak, but the picture I'm painting is a reality for a lot of Americans. To open up a dialogue about late-in-life care, I want to tell you a story that nearly ripped a family apart. After you read the story, I want you to ask yourself what you would do. Then, I'm going to leave you with a few questions that you should put on the table with your own family well before you retire.

Danielle and Amanda are sisters. They were close growing up, were maids of honor at each other's weddings. Their husbands, Dave and Lyle, were friends. Danielle developed Alzheimer's disease in her sixties. At first, it was manageable, but then it became apparent that she'd need around-the-clock care. Meanwhile, her husband, Dave, had made some bad late-in-life investments that drained their savings rather significantly. Still, they were able to afford a nice long-term care facility for Danielle while she was still lucid. Amanda and Lyle visited Danielle every weekend.

While Danielle and Dave had two kids, Amanda and Lyle remained childless. They loved the freedom that allowed them to work like crazy in order to save a bundle and retire early. They planned to travel and write, two of their passions, without worrying about money. Danielle and Dave never really had enough. Dave's employment was sporadic, and he liked to sink money into big dreams that never materialized. And Danielle often left the financial planning to him, since the kids were her primary concern. The sisters stayed close throughout their lives, despite their very different paths.

Eventually, Danielle's long-term care began to entirely drain Dave's savings. He began to ask his children, who did well in life, to pitch in a little for the monthly costs of keeping their mother in the home she'd come to love. But Danielle was also getting sicker. She was less and less aware of her surroundings and increasingly disappearing into that awful disease, which made it hard for her to even know who was visiting her anymore. The kids asked Dave to consider a more affordable facility. Dave, however, didn't want to move Danielle. After tapping his kids for as much as they could afford, he asked Danielle's sister, Amanda, to help. After all, the sisters were so close and she and Lyle had a very comfortable nest egg. Surely they could part with a few hundred dollars a month to subsidize Danielle's costs. That's all he was asking for.

Amanda and Lyle talked long into the night about it. They came to a painful decision. The next day, Amanda said no to Dave. They weren't willing to pay for Danielle to stay in that home. They suggested it was time for Dave to move her to the more affordable nursing home down the road—the one that accepted Medicaid.

It's an all-too-common story. You may be thinking that the problems started with Dave's bad investments. Maybe you think Amanda and Lyle were selfish. Danielle was her beloved sister, and what were they using their money for, anyway? Maybe you think Danielle's kids owed her more. Maybe the problem goes back even further, to Danielle, who, knowing how bad her husband was with money and investing, should have been setting aside her own funds for just such an emergency. Bad money patterns make themselves clear early on, and if they're not corrected, they only get worse. You can stay married to someone like Dave, but you have to work hard to extricate yourself financially, in the interest of self-preservation.

I am with Amanda and Lyle on this. I completely agree with their decision, a very difficult one. They have to think about their own late-in-life care. You may think they have a lot of money because they're only supporting themselves, but that's the problem. Unlike with Dave and Danielle, they don't have kids and grandkids who might be able to help out, drive them to the eye doctor, and pitch in financially now and again. They must take that into consideration long before they write a check to anyone, for anything.

As for Dave, you have to do what you can afford. Left with no other options, he applied for Medicaid; because of the couple's precarious financial situation, they were approved. Dave moved his wife to the nursing home Amanda and Lyle suggested. Luckily, the disease blunted some of the edges of her new reality, so she didn't mind living with roommates in a smaller, louder ward. Danielle died without knowing her family had been ripped apart over this.

Dealing with long-term care of our elderly is a decision that's always going to be fraught with emotions.

Money Mistake: You Haven't Set Anything Aside for Your Funeral

THE FIX: PREPLAN, EVEN IF YOU CAN'T PREPAY

The only industry more insidious than the wedding industry is the funeral industry. Both play heavily on your emotions at times when you need to be clear-minded and frugal. But the funeral industry is a special kind of evil, because wedding planning leaves a lot of time to think and second-guess every financial decision you make. When my mother died, it took us all by surprise. I was in shock, and that's the state most people are in when someone dies, even if it's expected. To say I regret not planning for my mother's funeral is an understatement. If you don't take on the planning yourself, you're putting your family through a wrenching experience at the worst possible time. When someone dies, thousands of dollars must be spent in a matter of hours. And, just as the cost of living will always increase, so, too, will the cost of dying.

The average funeral in this country costs $10,000. That covers everything from transporting the body and embalming or cremating, to the casket, ceremony, disbursements (newspaper notifications, flowers, refreshments, booklets), burial, and plot. Totals vary wildly from state to state, of course. In Washington, D.C., the Department of Human Services offers burial assistance of $850 for funerals that cost under $2,000; at the other end of the spectrum are funerals that cost upward of $30,000 because loved ones splurged on items like a stainless-steel casket. That certainly explains why "death care" is a $17 billion industry. But here are a few ways to save money when emotions are riding as high as the price points.

First, plan ahead, pay in advance (if you can), and avoid the heartbreak and headache that funeral planning inevitably brings. Got the money for a deluxe oak casket with bronze handles? Knock yourself out if that's what you really want. But I hope the knowledge that it's a phenomenal waste of money follows you into the sweet hereafter (talk about Ghost Money!).

In a time of grief, the first skill that goes out the window is decision-making, so it's always good to bring someone else, a trusted friend, with you when making arrangements. And remember, funeral directors are not counselors; they're businesspeople first and foremost. The best ones are good at comforting with one hand while cashing the check with the other. You need someone reliable on your side to help sort through the hundreds of questions and decisions you have to make. Tell your friend your budget before you go in, and allow that person to help you stick to it.

If the funeral home says you must buy a casket from their company, find another funeral home. The markup on an average coffin is between 300 and 500 percent, so you can always do better on price. The biggest waste is always the coffin, something seen for a couple of days and buried underground for the rest of its existence. You might not be in the headspace to haggle, but you can ask someone less connected to the deceased to help you source a cheaper coffin. And don't shy away from talking money and savings at a funeral. There is nothing more disrespectful to the dead than using the inheritance they intended as a proof of their love for you to line the pockets of strangers. I've made it clear to my family that if they waste a dime at my funeral, I'll personally haunt them for the rest of their days.

I said it in the wedding chapter, and I'll say it again: Flowers are a stunning waste of money, not to mention bad for the planet. It's never lost on me that most fresh-cut flowers are flown by plane from South America, only to end up in the ground a few hours later. If you must have flowers, buy wholesale flowers and have some friends arrange them. Believe me, your friends will be glad to help out during your time of need. Alternatively, skip the flowers and donate that money to a worthy cause. Most funeral homes have decorative urns with artificial flowers that fill out a room nicely.

10 Crucial Financial Questions You Must Ask About Late-in-Life Care

As with funerals, you must have those frank and open discussions about long-term care before you need it. But that begins with honest talk about current financial situations and future needs. So pour the coffee, pull out the financial statements, and put these questions on the table.

1. **How much money do you have, exactly?** Sometimes parents don't like to tell their children how much money they have. But if your children are your benefactors and/or your executors, they need that information. As long as you're cognizant that the money is still under your control and you can hire a lawyer to ensure it stays that way, tell them everything. In order to make sound decisions about late-in-life care, a realistic snapshot can be achieved only if all the numbers are on the table. Make sure you know where all the files and important papers are located. Remember, this is your money's last real purpose on this planet.

2. **Do you want to be resuscitated?** This is a really important question, and I hate to put a monetary value on such an

ethical conundrum, but you must consider that, in the event of a stroke or heart attack or other major life-and-death event, medical science can do a lot to sustain you. But you may suffer brain damage and be in a coma, after which you'll be hooked up to very expensive machines to help you live and breathe. Long-term care of the completely incapacitated costs a fortune. This is a very personal question, but one that should be discussed and answered as you begin to deal with aging family members.

3. **What kind of care do you expect?** This is a discussion that should happen years before its onset, preferably in your fifties, when you're at least a decade or two away from that inevitability. Because chances are, as you age, you're going to weaken, and you're going to need some form of long-term care eventually.

4. **Are you expecting to live with your children if you can't live independently?** If you're expecting to move in with them, you must discuss this now. Make sure there's a way to lift the financial burden if something like this happens. This might be the time to transfer wealth in exchange for long-term care provided by your kids. If you're fine with a nursing home, you should have that clearly spelled out.

5. **What are your financial expectations of family?** Do you expect your kids to foot the bill for some of your long-term care? I know a big Italian family who wanted to ensure their mother retired in relative luxury and agreed to pay for the very best the nursing home had to offer. There were nine brothers and sisters, all of whom contributed

to varying degrees. They decided that everyone would contribute proportionately to their income. So the son with the successful chain of furniture stores paid the most, because he could, and the daughter on a fixed income paid the least. But they all paid something.

6. **What will happen when you're less mobile?** Does the bathroom need retrofitting? How are you handling the stairs? There will also come a day when you can no longer drive and won't be able to transport yourself to and from appointments. Make sure you have money set aside to fit your living situation to your changing lifestyle. Being self-sufficient for as long as possible will stretch your savings.

7. **What other income or subsidies are you eligible for?** Do your research and find out what your insurance policy covers, what benefits you're eligible for—such as disability, housing, or funeral costs—or if you can collect your spouse's pension if he or she has passed away.

8. **Are you willing to move?** You might have to relocate to be closer to family as you need more and more of their help. Be open to that. Or, if finding housing in a cheaper city or country is possible, consider that as well.

9. **Are your papers in order?** Check your will, make any last-minute changes, and make sure you've assigned an executor you trust. Consult an estate-planning lawyer if need be. Also, are there safety deposit boxes or other accounts that you haven't mentioned?

10. **What do you want your financial legacy to be?** Do you have a trust? Who will have power of attorney if you are incapacitated? What are your wishes in that case?

Remember, you're going to have to answer every one of these questions at some point. And if you're the adult child of middle-aged parents, consider having these conversations now, when your folks are still lucid and well enough to have agency over their own decisions. Never lose sight of the fact that it's their money. You're just the shepherd. Give advice if you see fit, but don't expect anyone to take it.

Getting to "Enough"

I believe money makes life easier. But you might be surprised to learn that I don't think money necessarily makes life better. We probably all know miserable rich people. I certainly do. You couldn't pay me to live their lives. But the truly wealthy people I know, the ones with more than just money to account for their joy, seem to have one simple secret. You hear it over and over again. It is this: Even when I hardly had anything, I always had enough. When you get to a place of "enough," you will stop having money problems. Some people find that path spiritually, some through their families or community involvement, some through plain hard work and dedication. Some, like the folks in Debtors Anonymous, come to this place through awful financial strife. How you get to that place of "enough" is your own business. But you have to get there, or else, no matter how much money you have, it's never going to feel sufficient.

I've discovered that money is the most forgiving energy on the planet. The second you begin to make even the most minor positive adjustments to your spending, saving, or investment habits, money begins to flow back to you. And I believe you have a choice about how you spend your money. What you spend money on is the manifestation of that choice. As you've read in these pages, better choices mean more money. It is that simple. If you look at every financial transaction of your life as representative of the kind of person you are or want to be, a shift will happen.

Until you behave differently with money, nothing will change. Simply put, until you actually stop overspending, until you actually start saving and investing, you will never have enough of what you want. Another way to generate a sense of having "enough" is to cultivate gratitude for what you *do* have. This often comes naturally to people as they age, because they start to gain perspective. The things they thought were important when they were young just aren't that important anymore. They begin to feel gratitude for the things they do have, for the life they live, and for the time they can keep on living. I see that "attitude of gratitude" in people I admire—in my stepfather, George, and certainly in my mother when she was alive.

My parents weren't wealthy just in terms of money. They had a wealth of experience, a wealth of friends, and a wealth of love. And when I listened to those people in Debtors Anonymous, the ones on the road to financial recovery, they all had that same "attitude of gratitude" in common. There they were, broke and starting from scratch again, and yet they exuded hope. And by trying to help each other, they were taking the first steps toward real financial change.

The best part about getting older is this: If you've lived a full life, if you've made mistakes and learned from them, and if you're lucky enough to surround yourself with people who really know you and love you, something magical happens—material things no longer matter as much. What does begin to matter are the things in life that are free—things like love, respect, and integrity—and no amount of money can buy you those.

ACKNOWLEDGMENTS

When I was a young student in business school, Harry Lang, a professor, told me there was no substitute for experience. At the time, that meant nothing to me. Then came the real world, which hit me like a ton of bricks. Now I know he spoke with the wisdom granted only by the passage of time.

In my life, I have experienced great successes and catastrophic failures. I have lost millions and made them back. I have started many businesses, some of which died on the vine and others that I sold for billions of dollars.

It would have been impossible for me to write this book without the cumulative experiences of my journey. Along the way, I have learned lessons from the most vicious competitors, business partners, loyal friends, employees, brilliant investors, crafty politicians, and inspiring artists. Some of these men and women are close friends today; others I have not spoken to in years. Still, I have never forgotten the lessons these people have taught me. I would like to list all of their names here but practicality stops me, so instead, I acknowledge them knowing with certainty they know who they are. In a way, they wrote this book for me and I was just the scribe who inked the paper. I give them my thanks now.

Acknowledgments

I also want to give accolades to my literary collaborators, Lisa Gabriele and Bree Barton. The written word is permanent, and working with great artists like these makes it worth doing.

Finally, I wish to thank my parents, George and Georgette, who were my constant allies and advisors throughout my life. If it is the burden of parents to pass their knowledge to their children, then they can rest assured that their job is done and mine has just begun.

I wrote this book for anyone who wants to tap my database of experiences. I hope that this book helps those on their own journeys; after all, what else is there in life besides *Men, Women & Money?*

ABOUT THE AUTHOR

KEVIN O'LEARY is one of North America's most successful business entrepreneurs, as well as a star of ABC's *Shark Tank*. Kevin founded and built SoftKey (later called The Learning Company), a global leader in educational kids' software, and negotiated its sale to Mattel for $4.2 billion in 1999. Since then, he has successfully cofounded, funded, and sold numerous companies in a range of industries, including storage, entertainment, and finance. Kevin is the founder of O'Leary Fine Wines, an avid guitarist, and a photographer. Follow Kevin on Twitter @kevinolearytv or become a Facebook fan at Facebook.com/kevinolearytv.

I love great wine, and I never spend money
without looking for great value.

If you share these ideals, then I think you'll love
O'Leary Fine Wines as much as I do. Cheers!

HONEST · DIRECT

KEVIN

O'LEARY™
FINE WINES

Learn more at
kevinoleary.com/finewines